THE THRIVING EMPATH

A Survival Guide for Empaths to Becoming a Super Attractor, Discovering Inner Gifted Psychic Abilities, Set Boundaries with a Narcissist, And Reduce Anxiety

Melissa Gomes

>> https://smartpa.ge/MelissaGomes<<

© Copyright 2022 by Melissa Gomes

All Rights Reserved.

No part of this publication may be reproduced, distributed, or transmitted in any form or by any means, including photocopying, recording, or other electronic or mechanical methods, without the prior written permission of the publisher, except in the case of brief quotations embodied in reviews and certain other noncommercial uses permitted by copyright law.
Disclaimer: This book provides accurate and authoritative information regarding the subject matter. By its sale, neither the publisher nor the author is engaged in rendering psychological or other professional services. If expert assistance or counseling is needed, the services of a competent professional should be sought.

Table of Contents

TABLE OF CONTENTS	3
FREEBIES!	7
Bonus 1: Free Workbook - Value 12.95$	7
Bonus 2: Free Book - Value 12.95$	8
Bonus 3: Free audiobook - Value 14.95$	8
Join my Review Team!	8
For all the Freebies, visit the following link:	9
I'M HERE BECAUSE OF YOU ♥	10
CHAPTER 1: EMPATHS ARE BRAVE AND CONFIDENT	11
Standing Up for the Self	11
Let Yourself Be Heard	13
The Need for Solitude and Balance	15
CHAPTER 2: HOW TO CHANNEL YOUR ENERGY AS AN EMPATH	18
The Gift of Empathy	20
Empaths Feel Everything	21
Help Flows in an Empath's Core	22
Channeling Your Energy Pool	22
CHAPTER 3: HOW TO COPE WITH BEING AN EMPATH	24
Copying Strategies for Empaths	25
Have Fun With Your Creativity	25
Independency	26
Characteristics of an Inexperienced Empath	27
8 Self-Care Tips to Avoid burnout as a Highly Sensitive Person	28
Practice Yoga every day	29
Breathing technique fundamentals	30
Poses for releasing negative emotions in yoga	31
Your house is your haven.	32
CHAPTER 4: EMPATHS AND BOUNDARIES	35
Give Only What You Receive	35
Settings Boundaries is a Priority	36
Spend Time With the Ones Who Matter	37
Great Communication is Your Artillery	38
You are Your Superpower	39

SLEEP AND MEDITATE LIKE A PRO	39
BE A BODY AND MIND GYM RAT	40
SAYING NO IS A GOOD THING, TOO	41

CHAPTER 5: DIFFERENT PERSONALITIES IN EMPATHS — 43

SO WHICH ONE ARE YOU?	43
Extroverts: The Outgoing Ones	*43*
Ambiverts: The Bilateral Ones	*45*
Introverts: The Silent Ones	*47*
Omnivert: The Hot or Cold Ones	*48*

CHAPTER 6: HELPFUL ACTIVITIES FOR COPING EMPATHS — 51

READING	53
LISTENING TO MUSIC	53
LEARNING NEW LANGUAGES	54
PHOTOGRAPHY	54
COOKING	54
WATCHING MOVIES	55
WRITING	55
FOCUSING ON ART	55
GARDENING	56
EXERCISE	56
MAINTAINING A HEALTHY LIFESTYLE	57
ENGAGING IN HEALTHY SOCIAL ACTIVITIES	57
TRAVELING	57
MASSAGE THERAPY	58
GETTING ENOUGH SLEEP	58
MEDITATION	58
POSITIVE VISUALIZING	59
RECITING POSITIVE AFFIRMATIONS	59

CHAPTER 7: PREVENTING EMPATHS FROM EMOTIONAL OVERWHELM — 61

EAT THE RIGHT FOOD.	61
CLEANSE YOUR AURA.	62
PROTECT YOURSELF FROM OTHERS' ENERGIES.	62
CONSULT WITH YOUR ANCESTORS OR SPIRIT GUIDES.	64
GROUND YOURSELF.	65
YOUR PETS ARE THERE FOR YOU.	69
RELEASE YOUR STRONG EMOTIONS.	70

CHAPTER 8: FINDING COMFORT IN CONFUSING PLACES — 72

Good Experiences Will Do You Good	73
Choose What You See on Social Media	74
Be the Change You Want To See in Others	76
Perform One Random Act of Kindness Daily	78

CHAPTER 9: CAREER PATH FOR EMPATHS — 82

Empathy in Many Types of Work	82
Empathy and Creativity	83
Always a Helping Hand, Even at Work	84
Careers that Empaths Avoid	85
Empaths in Leadership Roles	87

CHAPTER 10: CENTER YOUR EMPATHIC SELF — 91

Center Yourself	91
Calling Divine Forces	95
Consciousness to Unconsciousness	96
Reach out to the Pros	99

CHAPTER 11: AN EMPATH'S HEALTHY DIET — 101

CHAPTER 12: GOOD-TO-KNOW STUFF FOR YOUR EMPATH CHILD — 104

How to Identify an Empath Child	104
Helping your Empath Child Manage Emotions	107

59 POSITIVE AFFIRMATIONS — 113

59 Affirmations for Empowering Empaths	113

FREEBIES! — 117

Bonus 1: Free Workbook - Value 12.95$	117
Bonus 2: Free Book - Value 12.95$	118
Bonus 3: Free audiobook - Value 14.95$	118
Join my Review Team!	118
For all the Freebies, visit the following link:	119

I'M HERE BECAUSE OF YOU 🖤 — 120

FREEBIES

AND

RELATED PRODUCTS

WORKBOOKS
AUDIOBOOKS
FREE BOOKS
REVIEW COPIES

HERE

HTTPS://SMARTPA.GE/MELISSAGOMES

Freebies!

I have a **special treat for you**! You can access exclusive bonuses I created specifically for my readers at the following link! The link will redirect you to a webpage containing all my books and bonuses for each book. Just select the book you have purchased and check the bonuses!

>> https://smartpa.ge/MelissaGomes<<

OR scan the QR Code with your phone's camera

Bonus 1: Free Workbook - Value 12.95$

This **workbook** will guide you with **specific questions** and give you all the space you need to write down the answers. Taking time for **self-reflection** is extremely valuable, especially when looking to develop new skills and **learn** new concepts. I highly suggest you *grab this complimentary workbook for yourself*, as it will help you gain clarity on your goals. Some authors like to sell the workbook, but I think giving it away for free is the perfect way to say **"thank you" to my readers**.

Bonus 2: Free Book - Value 12.95$

Grab a **free short book** with **22+ Techniques for Meditation**. The book will introduce you to a range of meditation practices you can use to help you develop your inner awareness, inner calm, and overall sense of well-being. You will also learn how to begin a meditation practice that works for you regardless of your schedule. These meditation techniques work for everyone, regardless of age or fitness level. Check it out at the link below!

Bonus 3: Free audiobook - Value 14.95$

If you love listening to audiobooks on the go or would enjoy a narration as you read along, I have great news for you. You can download the audiobook version of *my books* for **FREE** just by signing up for a FREE 30-day Audible trial! You can find the audio versions of my books (depending on availability) at the following link.

Join my Review Team!

Are you an avid reader looking to have more insights into spirituality? Do you want to get free books in exchange for an honest review? You can do so by joining my Review Team! You will get priority access to my books before they are released. You only need to follow me on Booksprout, and you will get notified every time a new Review Copy is available for my latest release!

For all the Freebies, visit the following link:

>> https://smartpa.ge/MelissaGomes<<

OR scan the QR Code with your phone's camera.

I'm here because of you 🖤

When you're supporting an independent author,
you're supporting a dream. Please leave
an honest review on Amazon by scanning
the QR code below and clicking on the "Leave
an Amazon Review" Button.

★★★★★

https://smartpa.ge/MelissaGomes

Chapter 1: Empaths are Brave and Confident

Empaths are sensitive souls who understand the damaging effects of conflicts. Even when their opinions are challenged, they avoid all forms of conflict; due to this reason, confidence should be practiced as this will help you in learning to handle any difficult situation that may come your way. Being an empath is not all fun and enjoyment; it also comes with its challenges. It is important to learn how to protect yourself from the harmful energies of others by learning how to block negative events from affecting you.

Empaths can be brave in facing challenges as they need to learn how to cope with the negative emotions of others. If you are an empath, you must learn how to block negative influences from affecting you.

Standing Up for the Self

People often misunderstand empaths, so they keep their gift to themselves. In reality, highly sensitive souls should be proud of their gift, and they should not doubt their talents in difficult times. Many people with empathic abilities are shy and reserved individuals, so they usually keep their feelings to themselves until they explode. Empaths must stand their ground for their well-being because being suppressed will only make them more upset. If they use their gift, they will no longer feel threatened and abused by others. As an empath, you must always stand up for yourself because being timid will only give you a hard time in life. If people try to take advantage of your kindness, then it would be best if you draw your boundaries firmly. People think empaths are weak and easily manipulated, so they take advantage of your generosity and kindness. In hindsight, the situation is quite the opposite: empaths are brave and confident; they consider what others need from them despite being taken advantage of.

Fortunately, there are techniques that you can use to improve your self-confidence and self-esteem. The correct amount of self-confidence is very important for successful empaths. Empaths can walk the fine line between letting the world know of their abilities and not exposing their gifts too widely. They often feel responsible for the actions of others around them, and others would take advantage of their abilities. It is normal to be afraid of the unknown; however, fear should not be your only motivation in life. Take pride in your gifts, which will make you a powerful individual. Other individuals will admire you and respect you because of your innate abilities. Your self-confidence will become the foundation of your personal and professional life. You will be motivated to work hard and use your abilities to achieve your desired goals in life.

In some cases, empaths let others exploit them, and this is due to a lack of confidence or self-esteem. It would help if you learned to value yourself, which will boost your confidence in your abilities. Many individuals are often afraid of negative energy; this often leads to confrontations. These confrontations may result in the loss of friends and the destruction of relationships. Sensitive souls are very good at reading people and situations; they can sense people's negative intentions during interactions. However, not all negative intentions are obvious to the naked eye; this is why empaths need to learn to be confident in their decisions and handle difficult situations.

Most empaths are mild-mannered, and you can establish confidence by standing up for yourself when necessary. Empaths often tend to trust too much; however, this can lead to many consequences in the long run. For instance, empaths may tend to trust individuals who break their hearts, or these individuals may be self-absorbed and manipulative. As a result, you will feel miserable and betrayed in the end because these individuals will use your weaknesses to hurt you emotionally or financially. Therefore, you must learn to protect your heart from dishonest individuals in your life; otherwise, you will become vulnerable to those commonly known as "energy vampires".

Being assertive can sometimes help empaths in establishing boundaries for others. It can teach them how to protect themselves from toxic individuals and environments. You do not have to be aggressive or loud when communicating your thoughts with others; you can express your feelings through actions instead. For instance, if you are unhappy with your children's behavior, you can sit them down and explain how you feel about them breaking the rules or doing the wrong things. If you want to teach your children a lesson, you could also take away their privileges like TV time or mobile phone time as a form of punishment. If you are in a relationship with an emotionally abusive partner, you should communicate your feelings to your partner openly and honestly instead of taking things personally. You can also practice empathy by putting yourself in your partner's shoes to understand them to feel better. This practice will give you more insight into your partner's behavior and allow you to deal with them more effectively. Some sensitive souls end up attracting people who are insensitive or negative. As an empathic soul, you should focus on the positive side of life.

Let Yourself Be Heard

Empaths are frequently trusted with people's issues because of their compassion and desire to satisfy others. However, this could leave them emotionally spent and unable to concentrate on their daily activities and unheard of their emotional needs.

Letting others know what you need will help your energy field. At first, it can feel uncomfortable, but as soon as you discover how much better you feel, it will start to seem natural to you. The truth is that your energy field is in tune with your needs and can help you recover from stressful situations quickly. If you learn to pay attention to your body and its subtle messages, it will better equip you to protect your mind from the adverse effects of negative emotions.

Emotional clutter can negatively affect your health, so you must learn how to clear your mind of negative emotions such as anger and resentment. Imagine a house with a chock full of items you do not need, which is piling up, filling the house with no room for you to sleep on; the same goes with your emotions. If you constantly feel angry and resentful, you can voice them out to a close friend and let them help you clear your mind of these negative emotions. Instead of venting your emotions to someone who may not be able to understand your frustrations, talk to someone who can relate to your situation and help you solve your problems. Letting yourself be heard at times can help empaths release bottled emotions and be free from negative thoughts; thus, you will be able to handle situations more calmly and effectively. This step also allows you to be filled with better and more positive emotions.

Learning to clear your mind is essential if you want to live a healthy and productive life. Negative emotions can affect your physical health as well as your mental and emotional health; therefore, you must learn to recognize these negative emotions when they occur. Clearing the mind is essential for eliminating emotional clutter; this is another reason you should practice mindfulness regularly. When you are stressed, allow your body to rejuvenate itself by relaxing in a quiet room while practicing deep breathing techniques for several minutes every day. In the following chapters, I have included some steps to help you achieve mindfulness.

Your family and friends should consider your personal space and honor your requests for privacy and trigger avoidance. You can do that by asking them not to bother you when you are busy; you can also politely ask them to stop asking you for help when they realize that you are busy or tired. You can also exercise a little discipline in responding to questions such as "How are you?" as many people do not realize how intrusive these questions can be. Still, they can be disruptive to an empath's energy field and trigger an emotional outburst from that person. A simple "I am fine" should be enough for friends to realize that you do not want to discuss your problems at the moment. When you are done with what you are going through, you can explain to the other person what you went through and share your feelings with them.

Some people around you will try to decide for you if they do not understand your goals, dreams, or abilities. Therefore, you must understand your strengths and weaknesses and let people know that you are in control before taking advice from the wrong people in your life. In addition, you will make mistakes in life, and you must learn from your experiences and be proactive in your decisions. An overabundance of negativity can drain your energy, so you must be willing to distance yourself from negative individuals and toxic environments as much as possible. Instead, surround yourself with positive individuals such as friends and family members who respect you for who you are. A peaceful environment is necessary to maintain a high energy level and focus.

The Need for Solitude and Balance

Empaths must learn how to manage their energy to avoid exhausting themselves. Many strategies will help you manage your energy field; however, one of the best things you can do is to become more aware of your body's signals and how your emotions affect your overall health. You do not have to wait for someone else to invite you to a party to enjoy yourself; in fact, parties can be exhausting for sensitive souls because a lot of negative energy surrounds them. If you have the energy to a party, by all means, do it; however, you should stay home and relax in a bubble bath or go for a walk in nature than go to a party or a nightclub. Socializing can be fun and relaxing for some sensitive souls; however, for others, it can be draining or even painful. Spending time with high-energy people without taking a break to relax can leave you feeling drained or exhausted.

Enjoying your hobbies can help you center your focus on what is around you rather than stress yourself out by dwelling on your thoughts. Getting plenty of rest will help you recharge your batteries so that you can be productive for the rest of the day, and going to bed early and getting at least seven hours of sleep every night will recharge your batteries for the next challenge.

Many people find relief in spending time with pets; some sensitive souls find that petting a cat or dog makes them feel better after a long day of work. Having pets can help empaths feel grounded and centered again after a stressful day, so you may want to consider getting a pet if you feel drained by being around other people for extended periods.

If you are always on the go, you might have trouble maintaining your energy level if you are always running from one thing to another. Even if you are an empath who has a lot of stamina, you need to take care of yourself as well because you may not realize when you are suffering from exhaustion until you are on the verge of getting sick. If you become ill from overexertion, you will not be able to finish your daily chores because you are sick in bed; therefore, it is important to practice self-care daily to ensure that you do not push yourself too hard for too long. If you do not prioritize your time well and do not take the time to relax, you will eventually burn yourself out and feel exhausted.

Remember not to work yourself to exhaustion regularly; instead, schedule regular breaks throughout the day where you can take a few minutes to rest and relax before going back to what you were doing. If you are in the habit of burning the candle at both ends and feeling drained at the end of every day, you might want to consider reducing your workload by delegating your tasks or managing your time in between.

Chapter 2: How to Channel Your Energy as an Empath

A true empath can tell when a person is being truthful or not, and this is by sensing the energy that surrounds the other person. If their energy matches their words, then they are telling the truth; however, if their words do not match their energetic state, they are not being truthful. Empaths can be extremely perceptive of other people's energy fields, and in exchange, they receive information about their emotional states, such as feelings of anxiety or depression. This ability is known as empathic accuracy. They can accurately read others' emotions through their body language and energy field. An empath is a person that can feel another's emotions as their own. This process is complicated as it is not as simple as picking up on another person's feelings but more like feeling those emotions from within them as well as from your own body. This process allows an empath to truly feel what others are feeling as if it were their own. They are often very good at reading people and predicting what they are about to do before they do it. They are sometimes known as psychics or intuitive.

Empaths are often very compassionate people as they are sensitive to the feelings and emotions of others and are very in tune with them; they feel the sadness and joy of others as if they were their own; they have empathy and compassion for other people, and often find themselves drawn to helping those in need. They can be very strong-willed and determined to help or guide someone when they are needed most. They often have a strong desire to heal the world or help others somehow. As true empaths are highly sensitive to others' feelings, they often find themselves deeply affected by the actions of others around them. Their emotions are affected greatly by others' actions, and selfish people take advantage of empaths for their gain. Their compassion can sometimes cause them to feel helpless at times as they find it difficult to say no to those who ask them for help, even when they are not in a state of mind to be able to help the person that is in need. They can sometimes feel overwhelmed by the emotional pain they absorb from others around them and feel helpless to help heal it.

Empaths often want to learn who they are and their purpose on earth. This stage triggers a spiritual awakening as they realize they are much more than the physical being empaths once thought they were. They begin to experience a burning desire to become more spiritually aware and explore their spirituality more thoroughly; they are on a quest for self-discovery. During this awakening period, an empath will begin to feel an inner peace that helps them gain perspective of their life and how they have been living it thus far. They will begin to understand who they truly are on a deeper level; empaths will discover their true purpose and why they were put on this earth in the first place. They will also begin to understand that all of life is connected; nothing is separate or isolated from one another; everything is connected on a spiritual level, and they will begin to sense more of this connection with each passing day.

While an empath's spiritual journey begins when they awaken to their true nature, it is far from over. Although they may believe they have achieved a certain level of understanding, their journey is not complete until they reach the final stage of their spiritual journey, which is enlightenment. An enlightened person is a true master at controlling their emotions and the energies that they emit into the world; they have mastered the art of unconditional love. They no longer judge others by their physical appearances or actions but by their essence; they see beyond the physical shell that others present to the world and truly see who people are inside. They can see past the darkness and the light within each soul. At times, they can even connect with the soul essence of every person they encounter in life, for they have learned to connect with all souls at once.

Some empaths can also send healing energies to people in need even when they are miles apart. They have learned to control this ability and use it for good instead of evil; they no longer need to hide their abilities from the world because they have mastered it and learned to use it to help others. Once an empath awakens from a traumatic event or experience, it shakes them up and causes them to question their life choices and how they have lived their lives up until now. Many undergo this awakening when faced with great personal loss, and from crumbling to almost nothing, they rise from the ashes as their renewed selves.

The Gift of Empathy

Some empaths take years to learn the art of giving without a gift. Once an empath learns this, they usually become a more giving and compassionate individual. With so much negativity in our world, it is difficult not to feel affected by what is happening around us. Being empathic is a gift we can use to help change the world for the better; it is a gift that we can all learn from and use daily to make our world a brighter place for all.

Not all people can understand another's point of view as easily as a truly empathetic soul can; this skill is something we should all learn to embrace and use more often in our daily lives. An empathetic person understands that they are not alone in the world. Even if they may feel alone, empaths understand how others are feeling deeply and are more sensitive to other people's emotions than the average person. Some are born with this gift, while others develop it as they age. It is still possible to develop empathy at any age if you open your heart to it and practice using it more often. We can all learn how to be more empathetic toward each other by learning how to control our emotions and be more accepting of other people's choices.

Empaths Feel Everything

Many empaths feel comfort in knowing there are others like them in the world; they understand that others feel the same as they do and that we connect with everyone in some way. They feel what other people are feeling, so it is easier for them to connect and relate to one another; they feel deeply, which is why they are so empathetic to everyone and everything around them. They can pick up emotions and vibes from other people's energy fields; it is like they are a mirror to this world and a reflection of all that is positive and negative about humanity. It is why it is so important to control your emotions and not lash out at others; you can cause more pain and suffering in the world, and this is not something you want to do. We can all learn from empaths, for they are so much more sensitive than the average person is; they are compassionate and understanding and understand that we are all connected in some manner.

The ability to express and understand your feelings is important, but being able to feel others' feelings is just as important for everyone to tap into. So many people live their life in emotional isolation; they are so closed off from their emotions that they block off from the world. An empath can usually feel how people around them feel, but they may not be aware of these feelings until they express them. Hence, learning how to control your emotion is so important.

Help Flows in an Empath's Core

An empath can often take on the pain of others to help them deal with their situations. This process can cause an empath to feel drained and sometimes depressed as they take on too much emotional pain that they cannot handle on their own; this causes them to take on more pain and exhaust themselves even more. Being an empath can be a gift, but it can also be a curse, too. It is challenging for the true empath to live in this world without having a breakdown at some point in their life due to taking on too much emotional pain from others.

If you are a true empath, you will find it difficult to live in the world without becoming depressed or affected. With all the events around us, it is natural to have these negative emotions from time to time. Still, when it affects you daily and causes you to suffer from depression, it is time to take some action to heal yourself and prevent yourself from breaking down emotionally.

It is normal for empaths to offer help to others but not always be able or willing to help themselves when they need it; this is when it becomes a problem. You need to be able to protect yourself from becoming overwhelmed. Giving others help is almost essential to empaths, for most of them experienced a point when no one was there to help them when needed. It was an empathic cry that others heard and has been their calling ever since; it is in their core to help others in need.

Channeling Your Energy Pool

Our body is a constant transformation of energy, and so is the rest of the universe. As we eat to fill our body's daily needs, we convert this into stored energy that we use in our daily needs. Our activities consist of intake and expel of energy and functions like clockwork. Empaths, having the gift of absorbing more emotional energy than others, can gather and store this energy from the environment and store it in their energy pool for use when needed. Through this process, an empath can heal themselves from the negativity around them and prevent themselves from taking on too much negative energy; in other words, they can use their powerful abilities to heal themselves. They can protect themselves from this by channeling their energy pool into healing their body instead of taking on the negative.

We can refill our energies through rest or relaxation. By giving yourself some downtime to recharge your batteries and relax, you can replenish your energy; it is important to do this regularly to prevent yourself from taking on too many negative energies around you daily. By learning to breathe properly and taking deep breaths several times a day, you can clear your mind of unnecessary thoughts and restore your body to its natural state of peace and calm. In the next chapters, I have included some steps for you to regain this peaceful state.

Chapter 3: How to Cope with Being an Empath

Living as an empath is difficult because everyone is sucking your energy, and you're constantly exhausted by it. Plus, you're often confused about your intense feelings and don't always know how to deal with them. But being empathic is a superpower. It's how you can feel others' emotions so deeply that you can relate to them and help them heal. Being an empath means you experience life deeper than most people. You understand people's emotions and reactions better, and you can tune in to the energy of everyone around you. As a highly sensitive person, you absorb energy and other people's emotions more easily than the average person. You often feel everything more intensely than those around you. Therefore, it is important to learn some coping mechanisms to help you deal with the stress of being an empath and dealing with all the negative energies you encounter daily.

As an empath, your life can be hectic sometimes. You might feel confused or overwhelmed by the energy you're taking in daily. Here are a few of the most common problems you might face as an empath. Empaths often struggle to maintain healthy boundaries because they get easily overwhelmed by others' negative energy or drained by excessive giving. Here are some ways to build and maintain **healthy boundaries**.

- Set limits with people who drain you and say no to requests that exhaust you.
- Practice self-care and ensure you get enough sleep and exercise to stay grounded and balanced.
- Avoid people who are constantly negative or draining.

- Create a morning routine that centers and grounds you each day.
- Learn to say no and avoid taking on other people's responsibilities.
- Focus on yourself so you can be the best version of yourself.

You can't stop being an empath, so here are some **unique coping strategies** to assist you.

Copying Strategies for Empaths
Have Fun With Your Creativity
Empaths are artists who enjoy drawing, painting, and dancing. They use their creativity to eliminate negative energy and create something beautiful to be proud of. Creativity is an escape from reality that allows you to escape into your world without worrying about what others think. Use your creativity to express yourself.

Painting and music can help you release negative emotions and energy that you may be holding in from everyday stress. Creative outlets like dance, music, art, and writing are also great ways to meditate and release stress when feeling overwhelmed. So try channeling your creative energy into something you enjoy to release stress and balance your emotions. If you like to dance, put on your favorite music and move your body to the rhythm of the music until you feel relaxed and refreshed. Using creativity as a coping mechanism can help you maintain energy levels as you deal with a stressful environment. You can try many creative activities, such as:

- Painting
- Writing
- Crafting

- Knitting
- Sewing
- Photography
- Cooking
- Gardening
- Dancing

Just do something you enjoy that helps you relax and center yourself when stressed; it will make a big difference in your life.

Independency
Empaths dislike their gift because it clutters their lives. They want to get away from the stress and negativity of other people and be alone so they can recharge their batteries in peace. Being alone helps you find your inner peace and balance your energies so that you can regain the strength to face the world again. To cope, you must find solitude to connect with your inner self. Introverts naturally use this coping strategy because they enjoy their own company. If you're an introvert, spend time alone to recharge your batteries and relax. If you find it hard to be alone, try meditation, yoga, or just taking a walk in nature so you can get in touch with your inner self. Introversion can help you find tranquility amid chaos because it allows you to be alone with your thoughts.

For empaths, this strong desire to assist others can become compulsive, leading to co-dependency. Co-dependency is when a person's satisfaction is derived from their ability to please and assist others at any cost, which creates an unhealthy relationship for both parties. As an empath, you spend a lot of time around others, so avoiding other people's drama or negative vibes is hard. However, you should try to avoid co-dependent relationships at all costs; they're exhausting and make you unhappy. Seek independency to feel free again. It will help you build healthy boundaries and take care of yourself to live a balanced life. Make time for your friends, family, and partner, but make sure you also take time for yourself to recharge your batteries and restore your energy reserves regularly. If you feel lonely, spend some time with a pet or talk to a friend on the phone to get the support you need. Going outside for fresh air can also work wonders to calm you down and clear your mind so you can reset and start fresh again.

Characteristics of an Inexperienced Empath

You can easily spot an inexperienced empath because of their low self-esteem and confidence. Empaths are often too shy to speak up or defend themselves in an argument because they fear what others will say about them. This tendency makes them unable to stand up for themselves and demand respect from others. If they're taken advantage of, they have difficulty asking for help because they fear rejection. They feel they need to care for everyone and everything around them but can never take care of themselves. These behaviors stem from their inability to self-advocate and accept help when needed.

The following are some of the characteristics of an inexperienced empath:

- Feeling responsible for the decisions of others
- Feeling obligated to assist others
- People in need are drawn to them
- A lack of self-control
- Oversensitivity to other people's moods, gestures, and even scents
- A tendency to take on other people's problems as their own
- An inability to say "No" to anything
- A lack of personal boundaries

- Difficulty saying what they need, want, or feel
- Overusing energy by helping others and forgetting about themselves
- Problems concentrating and making decisions
- Feeling tired and overwhelmed easily
- Making rash decisions and acting in haste
- Falling for every sob story
- Listening to others too much

All the above are the main signs of an inexperienced empath who cannot say "No" to anyone around them. This type of behavior is very draining and can lead to burnout if you spend all your time taking care of others without taking care of yourself. These characteristics are common among untrained empaths and often evolve into more serious issues like anxiety, depression, and co-dependence. To avoid burnout, use the following strategies:

8 Self-Care Tips to Avoid burnout as a Highly Sensitive Person

- **Find a trusted friend you can confide in and discuss your problems.** They might be able to give you advice on how to approach people in certain situations or help you say "No" when needed.
- **Accept that you're not perfect and that asking for help is okay.** Asking for help is not a sign of weakness; it's a sign of strength.
- **Stop being afraid to say no and stand up for yourself when appropriate.** You need to develop healthy boundaries so that other people won't take advantage of you. Remember: You can't make everyone happy all the time. If you try, you'll end up exhausted and feeling unfulfilled. It's better to focus on yourself and your needs instead.

- **Write down all the things you do for other people and then prioritize them.** You wouldn't believe how few people appreciate everything you do for them. After prioritizing everything you do for others, ask yourself, "Can I do less or delegate to others?"
- **Ensure you're eating well**, getting enough rest, and getting regular exercise. The best way to recharge your energy is to spend time alone, so avoid spending too much time with people who drain your energy instead of charging you up.
- **Don't suppress your feelings.** Instead, learn to express yourself by talking calmly and using "I" statements when describing your feelings, instead of saying "You" statements such as "You did this to me." This practice will help keep you calm and collected and avoid saying things in anger or out of frustration.
- **Learn to take little daily breaks to relax and recharge your energy.** It might not be easy initially, but you'll get used to it the more you practice. You can even set your watch to go off every hour as a reminder to stop and take a break for a minute or two to relax and take a refreshing breath. This practice is particularly helpful if you feel overwhelmed with work or want to fight off feelings of depression.
- **Spend more time in sunlight.** Sunshine helps keep the body and mind healthy by improving mental clarity, protecting your nervous system, and boosting your Vitamin D levels. If possible, try to have your meals outdoors and plant some indoor plants like Aloe Vera to brighten up your office or home.

Practice Yoga every day

Yoga is a powerful tool for releasing negative energy and stress from the body so you can stay balanced and healthy. Practicing yoga regularly will help you build physical strength, increase flexibility, reduce muscle tension, improve posture, and calm your mind. You'll also get a restful night's sleep, which will help you recharge your batteries so you can be at your best the next day. Regular yoga practice will help you maintain a positive attitude and avoid stress-induced illnesses such as hypertension, heart disease, and diabetes.

Here are **seven reasons why you should include yoga in your self-care routine:**

1. Helps you keep your energy high and your emotions under control.
2. Helps you stay calm and centered so you can stay in charge of your emotions and whether you feel energized or drained.
3. It weakens destructive emotional patterns such as anger, jealousy, frustration, and worry so that you can remain calm during challenging or stressful circumstances.
4. Awakens powerful positive emotions like joy, peace, and happiness that can counter negative emotions and fill your mind with positive thoughts.
5. Helps to consciously overcome emotional habits like dwelling on the past, worrying about the future, or feeling frustrated
6. Promotes positive affirmations so you can reframe negative thoughts to increase your confidence, self-esteem, and ability to handle adversity.
7. Enhances creative visualization so you can envision yourself being successful in your personal or professional life.

Breathing technique fundamentals
Breathing techniques are important for controlling your emotions and staying calm under pressure. Practicing deep

abdominal breathing when you feel angry, frustrated, or stressed will help restore your energy and boost your focus so you can overcome any challenge you face. To have a good breathing technique, you should:

- Cross your legs and sit on the ground.
- Take a deep breath and close your eyes.
- For four seconds, hold your breath.
- Exhale for four seconds.
- Repeat for five minutes.

Poses for releasing negative emotions in yoga

Certain poses help you release your body's negative emotions such as anger, fear, anxiety, and frustration so you can stay healthy. Here are some of the best yoga poses for releasing negative emotions:

1. **The Plank Position**: This pose is excellent for reducing anger and frustration and helps you regain your focus and confidence. To do this pose, lie down on your stomach with your palms facing the ground beneath your shoulders, keeping your elbows directly under your shoulders. Keep your legs and feet together, and press your body up so your toes can reach the floor. Hold this position for five breaths to release negative emotions from your body. You can also do this pose on your forearms if you're a beginner.

2. **Dog Facing Upwards**: If you want to release tension from your neck and upper back, this is the pose you need to try. To do this pose, lie down on your back with your knees bent, feet flat on the floor, and arms by your sides. Place your hands behind your head with your elbows bent at a right angle. Lift your hips off the floor and raise your head so that your chin touches your chest.

3. **Pose with an Angle:** This is an advanced position requiring strength and flexibility in your body. To make this position work, start on your hands and knees with your wrists directly under your shoulders, knees directly under your hips, shoulders directly over your wrists and hips, and head aligned with your spine. Next, lift your knees off the floor and put the soles of your feet together on the floor. Raise your arms straight out in front of you while pressing firmly into the ground with the heels of your feet. Pull your navel in towards your spine as you lengthen the back of your neck, keeping the front of your torso long.

Your house is your haven.

Your personal space should make you feel safe, and the mood and atmosphere of your home should reflect how you feel on the inside.

If you are dissatisfied with your living situation, you may need to make some changes.

- A cluttered home can make you feel exhausted and helpless.
- A clean home makes you feel healthy, calm, and in command.
- House cleaning releases positive energy.

Clutter restricts positive energy flow in your home, resulting in exhaustion, stagnation, and exasperation.

- You will become more vibrant when you create harmony and order in your home. Clutter removal eliminates imbalances and blockages in your personal space.

- You will break bad habits and establish new ones by cleaning the house and watching TV on the couch rather than the bed.
- Your problem-solving abilities will improve.
- You will have more free time.
- If you clean up your bedroom, you will sleep better and have more time.
- You'll also save time if you don't have to search through a stack of items to find something.
- Your health will improve when you are surrounded by order and cleanliness.
- You can spend less money on cleaning and more time enjoying yourself.

If you want to improve how you live at home, use these ideas to make your living space a place of tranquility and relaxation.

- 1. **Clean Your House in One Place**: I like to start cleaning my bedroom and then move on to the living room. Cleaning one room at a time will help you thoroughly eliminate dirt and grime from each room of your home.
- 2. **Use Chemical-Free Cleaning Products**: Harsh chemicals can negatively affect your health. Use natural cleaners like vinegar, lemon juice, and baking soda to clean your house. You can make your cleaning solutions or buy chemical-free cleaners at the grocery store.
- 3. **Get Rid of Papers and Piles**: Papers and piles can create chaos in your home. Piles of mail, bills, newspapers, magazines, and other papers can make it difficult to get things done.
- 4. **Organize Your Closet**: To keep your closet organized, put similar items together by color or size and put them back in your closet after you've worn them.

- 5. **Apply Feng Shui in Your Room**: If you haven't heard of Feng Shui, it's an ancient Chinese art that organizes and energizes your home by giving it energy.
- 6. **Use Essential Oils**: Some essential oils have therapeutic properties and can improve your mood in your home without using harmful chemicals. Lavender, frankincense, peppermint, rose, and rosemary essential oils are good choices.

A clear space provides a sense of certainty and clarity, allowing you to concentrate on the present moment.

Chapter 4: Empaths and Boundaries

Empaths are known to define boundaries for self-preservation and to recharge their depleted energy. These boundaries help them stay grounded and maintain a sense of balance with their world. An empath's purpose is to use their intuition to help them guide others in the right direction, but when an empath uses their energy to help others without recharging, they risk being drained themselves. Their energy is pulled away from their well-being, causing further stress and confusion in the relationship. There are a few steps to preserve your energy as an empath and set limits for people who want to abuse your empathy.

Give Only What You Receive

An empath must balance giving and receiving to be healthy, happy, and fulfilled in their relationships. Being in an emotionally abusive relationship can be difficult for just about anyone. When an empath is in an emotionally abusive relationship, however, it can put them at an even greater risk of becoming depressed and losing their sense of self-worth during the whole ordeal.

Because many empaths give so much of themselves to everyone else, it can be especially difficult to realize that it is okay to receive support from those around them. They feel ashamed or guilty about asking for assistance and often feel like they should be able to handle everything on their own. Giving what you only receive sets the balance to equilibrium. Empaths should remember to focus on their own emotional needs before worrying about the well-being of others around them.

Even though an empath's purpose is to help others in their time of need, they can sometimes put the needs of other people ahead of their own. As a result, they may unintentionally be giving too much of their time and energy to the people in their lives. Setting boundaries with others can help an empath protect their energy from being drained by other people.

Settings Boundaries is a Priority

Empaths find it difficult to set boundaries because they don't like to upset, hurt, or offend anyone. By avoiding setting boundaries, empaths allow other people's negative circumstances into their lives. In addition, they are usually the support system in their friends' lives, which makes it especially hard for them to set boundaries with their loved ones. They are so used to taking on the responsibility of helping and caring for others that they often forget to take care of themselves first. To properly recharge their drained energy and become socially healthy again, an empath needs to learn how to set boundaries in their relationships so that they don't become so exhausted that they no longer have the energy to care for others.

Setting boundaries isn't about taking anything away from others; it's simply about balancing relationships so that everyone receives equal amounts of love and attention. Learning to set boundaries doesn't mean an empath is selfish or self-centered; it's about taking care of themselves so they can take care of others without feeling drained. A good way for empaths to set boundaries and protect their energy without feeling guilty is by setting aside time for themselves. Allowing a few minutes of their time for themselves each day can help an empath recharge their drained energy and remind them that they are worthy of love and care, too.

Spend Time With the Ones Who Matter

Another way for an empath to recharge is to spend less time with people who drain their energy and more time with people who energize them. Sometimes this means having to remove themselves from toxic relationships and spending time alone so that they can regroup and find new people who support and nurture them. Some empaths recharge their energy by spending time with their closest friends or relatives every day. Whichever way works best for each person will help ensure that they don't become overtaxed and burned out.

Each relationship empaths have is different and requires a different amount of energy to maintain. An empath needs to define these different relationships and learn how much time and energy they require to stay centered and grounded. As an empath, it's important to become honest about your energy needs and learn how to meet them healthily without taking on other people's energies too deeply.

Invest wisely in people. Some people won't listen to your advice and will continue down the same path they're on now, and that's fine because some people are just not meant to change or learn lessons, in which case they aren't worth your time anyway. Focus on those who you know are willing to listen and learn. Empaths have limited energies and sometimes can only accommodate several people at a time. This limitation leads others to think you have something against them when in reality, you're just trying to focus on the people who care for you the most. Trust your gut instincts and stay away from anyone who makes you feel uncomfortable or makes you question your worth as a person. Don't lose yourself in relationships.

Stay away from parasites. Empaths attract the wrong kind of people, so trust your instincts. As strong as empathy is, it's not strong enough to put you on an emotional train track with someone who isn't willing to put forth the effort to try and maintain their sanity and stability in life. Save your energy for people who care about you enough to help you grow as a person. Parasites can lead empaths down a dark path as they feed off of a person's emotions and are more interested in feeding off others' emotions than in their own. Empaths are sensitive souls who can feel what other people feel on a very deep level. If they haven't learned to protect themselves from absorbing the emotions of others, they can easily become overwhelmed with negative emotions and feel completely drained of energy.

Great Communication is Your Artillery

When speaking to someone about how you are feeling, use the right language. By learning to express your emotions clearly, you are communicating your needs to others in a less confusing way and easier to receive. Assertive communication is also useful when setting boundaries. Instead of allowing other people to walk all over you, learn to clearly state your needs to them so that they understand what is expected of them in the future. Empathy is a powerful tool that benefits everyone; however, it is important to learn how to balance your empathy with the needs of others so that you can avoid taking on too much of their negativity and becoming overwhelmed in the process.

When you learn to communicate your needs without losing your sense of self, you demonstrate that you value your relationship enough to take care of it. It also shows the other person that you are willing to take responsibility for your part in the relationship. By staying strong and clear in your communication, you can help your partner understand what they need to do to change and better the relationship for both of you. Use Your Intuition Because your intuition becomes stronger the more you use it, it's important to learn to recognize when it is telling you something. This takes practice; however, with time, you will find it easier to trust your intuition and use it as a guide to achieving your higher self.

You are Your Superpower

Empaths often believe they are responsible for how other people feel, but remember that you are only responsible for how you feel. When helping others through their problems, it is important to remind yourself that you cannot solve all of their problems for them. It's not your job to change people; it's your job to show them the way and provide support during their journey. Empathy can be draining when overused or channeled the wrong way, but it can be a wonderful gift as you can help people around you in their healing process.

Practicing empathy doesn't mean that you have to deal with everyone else's problems; it just means that you take the time to show people that you care about them enough to help them through their challenges. To get the most out of your empathic skills, remember to take time for yourself and surround yourself with those who uplift and support your energy. Use your intuition to help you identify the right people to be in your life and create strong and healthy boundaries so that you can protect yourself from too much negativity.

Sleep and Meditate Like a Pro

The importance of sleep is not limited to just rejuvenating the body. A well-rested mind works faster and better than a mind stressed by work and other life stresses, to which empaths are sensitive. Not getting enough sleep causes the body to crave more food and stimulants to stay awake; eventually, this causes the body to become susceptible to poor sleep patterns. If getting a full night of sleep is hard for you, try removing all electronics from the bedroom a few hours before bed; this will help signal your body that it is time to go to sleep rather than stay up working or surfing the internet.

If you're finding it difficult to turn off your mind at night, try practicing meditation before you go to bed; this can help clear your mind of all the thoughts and stressors from the day so that when you lay down to sleep, you will be fully relaxed. Getting a good night's rest will ensure you wake up feeling refreshed and ready to face a new day.

Setting your home with a dedicated sacred space, an altar, or simply a corner with items that can ground you can help you regain your lost energy. Some empaths embraced using crystals and other metaphysical tools to help them healthily regulate their empathic energy. Crystals have been used for thousands of years by shamans and healers to help ground spiritual energy and channel it into the body to provide healing for the physical body and emotional healing for the soul. Crystals are said to provide a sense of grounding and balance when used in conjunction with meditation and prayer. These tools can help ground energy within the body to prevent excess energy from flowing outwards.

Be a Body and Mind Gym Rat

Exercise is a great way to relieve stress and relax the mind. It can also help to boost energy levels, improve mood, and reduce feelings of depression. Find a type of exercise that you enjoy and do it regularly: walking, jogging, swimming, biking, or others.

Empaths tend to exercise less than the average person due to their energy-draining qualities; however, staying active is one of the best ways to keep yourself healthy, alert, and happy. The most important thing to remember is to get out of your comfort zone now and then to remain energized and balanced. Empaths can often get stuck in a rut with their daily routines and forget that there are other things they can do to help them relax, reduce stress, and stay energized throughout the day. Try a new exercise routine with a friend or try something new with your workouts; this will help you develop new hobbies and increase your overall well-being.

If you wish to exercise mentally, you can find hobbies like enrolling in an acting class, painting, or dancing. These types of activities will help get you out of your head and into the moment so that you can focus on something else for a while. No matter what type of exercise you choose to do, be sure to make it a priority; if you don't make time for it, you won't do it. Setting boundaries to how you spend your time helps you stick to your schedule and gives you something to work toward each day. One of the benefits of being an empath is that you learn to understand and recognize your energy levels; however, it's just as important to pay attention to how other people are feeling to get an idea of their needs. Always be aware of how you feel both physically and mentally; this means that you need to be in tune with your own body and pay attention to your emotions and physical signs like headaches, fatigue, cramps, or others.

Push yourself to do things you are not comfortable with or don't think you would be capable of achieving. Doing so will help you embrace extroverted traits such as enjoying adventure and novelty. Challenge yourself daily with something new - even the smallest action will help you stay energized throughout the day and help you see the world in a new way.

Saying No is a Good Thing, Too

Learning how to say no can be difficult for empaths because we often feel compelled to help others even when we don't want to. For empaths, saying no drains their energy and makes them more susceptible to burnout. When something comes up that they aren't willing to participate in or feel overwhelmed by your responsibilities, they need to learn to say no and set boundaries for themselves.

Saying no can be very difficult; however, it is necessary if you want to keep your energy up and feel happy at the end of the day. Saying no to one thing is easier than saying no to many other things; when you feel like saying no to something or someone, give yourself some time to think about what you want to say before you say it. Practice your refusals; pretend that you are speaking in a normal conversation and respond as you normally would. The more you practice saying no, the easier it will become for you. Remember that you don't need to say yes to every request or opportunity that comes your way; rather, pick the things that excite you the most and make you happy. By saying yes to only the things that matter to you, you will improve your overall well-being and enjoy things that truly bring you happiness in life.

Chapter 5: Different Personalities in Empaths

Although having alone time is one of the traits that describe empaths in general, ambiversion and extroversion are also features of many empaths, also known as "highly sensitive people". They instinctively understand others and are easily influenced by others. In adolescence and adulthood, they may experience bouts of overactive enthusiasm. These are their natural way of expressing ideas, so people around them are always affected by them negatively. These ambivert and extrovert empaths feel a need to be surrounded by people and socialize. When they feel too much negativity or criticism, they withdraw from the world and retreat into themselves like a turtle hiding back in its shell. Over time, they become depressed and need a lot of rest to recover their energy, just like introverts.

So Which One Are You?

Their emotional experience defines a person's behavior, which ultimately affects how they feel and act. People are born with their own set of temperaments and personality characteristics. A few commonalities define empaths from the rest of the population, but not all of them fall into the same category. Knowing about them, you'll become more aware of how you react to situations and how other people affect you. The more common your behaviors are, the more aware you are of them, and the more empathy you can show others.

Extroverts: The Outgoing Ones

Extroverted empaths are friendlier than their introverted counterparts and rarely suffer from loneliness or boredom.

They are also more organized than introverts and are good at managing their time efficiently. Empaths are sensitive to their surroundings, so they, in turn, become even more social if they are around negative people constantly. They may be easily distracted by negative people around them and lose focus. They may even lose motivation to work or study due to stress from the constant flow of negativity from their peers. These individuals usually enjoy group activities more than solitary activities, especially when they are in the company of other people who share the same interests as them.

Empaths who are extroverts are bubbly and energetic because they like being around people and interacting openly with them. They can even talk for long periods without getting tired because they are good conversationalists who love entertaining others with interesting stories and anecdotes. They are excellent at listening and observing because they understand that it is through their actions that people can get what they want in life. They remember what people say to them and others for future reference. Their ability to listen and observe enables them to understand the world around them better so they can make better decisions on things related to their profession or personal affairs.

Regarding personal matters, extroverted empaths usually initiate a conversation rather than wait to be asked first because they are recharged when they are with their friends and meet new people all the time. They are very communicative and love to be in the middle of all activities with their friends because being the center of attention is how they thrive. They are optimistic people and believe that they can positively influence others, which makes them believe that everyone can be great friends with everyone despite their differences in upbringing and culture.

As outgoing empaths, they are sympathetic, kindhearted individuals who love to help people in need and are less apprehensive about approaching them. Their positive outlook makes them think that everything they do is the right thing, so they often get disappointed when their expectations are not met because of unrealistic expectations from others. They are energetic and passionate individuals who can talk to anyone without batting an eyelid. But their caring nature sometimes gets these empaths into bad relationships because they need to please everyone else instead of themselves. They often sacrifice their happiness just to satisfy someone else's needs and avoid conflict in their relationships. Their friends often find themselves in the middle of disagreements caused by their selflessness and their efforts to please everyone around them. Extroverted empaths have certain emotional triggers that can influence their actions. They may suddenly lose interest in things they are passionate about because they become too distracted by negative vibes coming from those around them. Or they may get upset when they don't receive positive feedback from those around them, causing them to lose focus and get distracted from their goals in life. Nevertheless, extroverted empaths mote better than others socially because their emotions are out in the open for everyone to see. They also tend to be more expressive of their emotions than others because of their need to be sociable.

Ambiverts: The Bilateral Ones

Ambivert empaths are those who exhibit both introverted and extroverted personalities. They tend to prefer being around people but also require being alone occasionally. They show emotions differently from introverts and extroverts. They may appear calmer outside but may internalize their emotions more than extroverts do. They are also less tolerant of criticism than extroverted empaths. This behavior stems from their need to be perfect in everything they do to impress and avoid criticism from others. But they often expect too much from others, so they are often emotionally turned down when they do not get what they anticipate from people around them.

As ambiverts, empaths are more in control of their emotions because they are more aware of them than introverts and can regulate them in different situations. They can change their behavior to suit their environment when necessary because they better understand the needs of those around them. For example, they can turn from an outgoing person to an introverted one if they feel uncomfortable in a situation or do not want to draw attention to themselves. They also tend to be less affected by external stimuli such as noises, smells, and tastes, making them seem calm and relaxed to those around them. They have strong emotions, but they are more reserved in expressing them because they do not want to hurt the feelings of the people around them. They rely on their intuition more than intellect when making decisions because they do not enjoy analyzing situations or other people's motives.

Ambiverts are often accused of not having clear goals and of making impulsive decisions because their actions may seem contradictory to their behavior most of the time. But these are often assumptions based on the behavior of extroverts and introverts. It is very difficult for people to make assumptions about an ambivert because what they do and feel are not always the same. They can be confident one moment but sad the next because they are always aware of other people's feelings. This sudden switch makes them seem unpredictable to others and sometimes makes them seem like they have mood swings.

Although they may seem calmer than introverts or extroverts, ambivert empaths do feel emotional pain on the inside. Still, they have a hard time expressing it because they are afraid of being rejected. They often bottle up their feelings inside to avoid hurting or upsetting people. However, this can lead to depression or other mental disorders like bipolar disorder later in life, so ambiverts need to learn to express their emotions early to empower them. Because they prefer to be in control, ambiverts are often perfectionists who strive to do the best they can in everything they do to achieve their goals in life. They are good leaders and know how to motivate others, especially their team members, to achieve their objectives.

Introverts: The Silent Ones

Introvert empaths are those who prefer spending time alone and have difficulties expressing themselves to others verbally. They often hide their emotions and do not let anyone see their weaknesses or imperfections because they fear rejection or humiliation from others. Although they may appear calm on the outside, they are highly intuitive and sensitive to the feelings of others, which can sometimes cause them to be overwhelmed or hurt by the emotions of others. They are often perceived as quiet and distant individuals by others, which can make them seem cold and unapproachable at times.

Because they are not good at expressing their emotions and dislike socializing, introverts often find it difficult to open up to others and form close relationships. They do not like receiving compliments or making small talk with others because they tend to focus more on what they should be doing instead of what they are doing now. Because of this, they can sometimes be perceived as rude or unwelcoming by others because they do not like talking much and do not open up easily to others. They experience strong emotions, but they do not express them openly because they are uncomfortable with being judged by others and rejected.

Many introverts are naturally shy or reserved because of their fear of rejection from others, but they can be more pleasant if they get along with their friends or family members well. This is because such relationships give them a sense of security and allow them to feel comfortable sharing their thoughts, feelings, and experiences without feeling judged or criticized by others. They also tend to be excellent listeners and care for those they love and cherish. Because empaths are sensitive to the needs of others, they tend to love taking care of their loved ones. They can easily sense when someone is unhappy and try to comfort them to make them feel better. They want to be close to their loved ones so they can be there for them when they need emotional support.

Since they are often very attached to their loved ones, introverted empaths may even find it difficult to let them go, especially when they are facing a difficult life situation. Introverts often keep their problems to themselves because they do not like to share them publicly with strangers. Like other empaths, they are prone to depression and other mental disorders such as anxiety disorder if they do not learn how to deal with their emotions properly. Their desire to be perfect may also cause them to overwork themselves and put too much pressure on themselves to get things done on time, especially if they have a deadline to meet at work. This notion of life can leave them physically and mentally exhausted, resulting in physical and mental health problems later in life. So introverts need to take a step back and take time to relax and recharge whenever they feel overwhelmed by their responsibilities, may it be at work or at home. Recharging helps them to reduce stress and relax their minds as well as their bodies.

Omnivert: The Hot or Cold Ones
While ambivert empaths have both introverted and extroverted traits, omnivert empaths tend to use either personality trait depending on their situation. Omniverted empaths can easily adapt to whatever environment they find themselves in and are

very flexible in dealing with their problem. They can be easily angered in certain situations. Nevertheless, they can be cool and calm in the next moment because they are used to adapting to different situations, and they can handle different emotions. So what makes them so versatile? They can do this because they have developed very strong intuition that allows them to understand what is going on in their minds and the lives of those around them. This trait allows them to become more self-aware and intuitive of others' feelings and emotions when they interact with different people in their daily life.

Sometimes, they may find certain situations difficult to handle because of their extreme sensitivity. In these cases, they may keep their emotions in check to avoid exposing themselves to negative emotions such as sadness, anger, and frustration. It can cause them to be perceived as detached individuals by others, but they normally just want to remain objective and not let their feelings cloud their judgment when making decisions. These individuals are good leaders because they can lead people well in any situation due to their strong versatile intuition and leadership qualities.

Omniverted empaths also have no problems communicating with other people as they have developed very good verbal communication skills that allow them to express themselves clearly and effectively to those around them. They are not afraid to speak up and share their opinions with other people because they believe that honesty is the best policy when it comes to communication. Despite this, they are open to new ideas and ways of thinking that can help them improve their problem-solving abilities. Omniverts are open-minded individuals who value knowledge and wisdom above anything else. They are very wise of their surroundings and can make decisions very quickly without overthinking things too much.

Distinguishing different personalities of empaths can help empower them to take charge of their lives and make better choices for themselves. Knowing more about their personality type can help them understand their strengths and weaknesses, so they can manage them properly in the future.

Chapter 6: Helpful Activities for Coping Empaths

In previous chapters, empaths are discussed as having coping mechanisms to regain their drained energy. These steps help empaths stay calm and positive and control their energy drain. When an empathic person is faced with a situation that exhausts them, they are taught to mentally "go away" from it for a while. Spending time in solitude allows them to rejuvenate their strength and ability to handle the situation. Being an empath is not being weak or allowing people to take advantage of you; it just means that you possess a heightened sense of feeling and understanding of other people's emotions and your own. An empath is also someone who understands how others are feeling because of their emotions and empathy for others' feelings. People who are not empaths may learn how to control their emotions, but for sensitive souls, this is more difficult, and they may feel emotionally overwhelmed at times, especially with loved ones.

Empaths are highly intuitive to their surroundings. They tend to feel what is going on in a room and pick up on the mood of the people there before they speak a word or show emotion. These feelings of being "on edge" all the time can be draining if nothing is done to control them or deal with them accordingly. Emotional control may seem impossible for some because being empathic means that your emotional body is heightened. Anything can cause you to feel overwhelmed. Because empaths are highly sensitive, they easily pick up on the emotions of others around them, which might affect them physically and emotionally. Feeling other people's emotions can cause one to feel depressed or overwhelmed, causing one to experience a mood disorder or even physical illness. Some people who are sensitive to their surroundings may deal with symptoms of anxiety, insomnia, depression, or fatigue because empaths are constantly aware of other people's feelings and are in tune with their feelings. For sensitive souls who experience "phantom pain" when others hurt themselves, this can be completely overwhelming because of the pain they cause to others without even realizing it. Empathy is a natural human trait that everyone has to some degree. For sensitive souls, this is what makes them so caring and empathetic towards others in need.

Empathetic people towards others in need can positively influence empaths. While this may apply to some, most empaths tend to become negatively influenced by those who don't care about anyone else's needs but their own. Due to being so empathetic, many sensitive souls can feel trapped between wanting to help those in need and feeling helpless. They cannot offer much to help because they are too exhausted from the draining situation. Finding a hobby that you enjoy is key, especially if you suffer from depression or anxiety, because your hobby should be something you look forward to doing instead of dreading it.

Understanding other people's pain and wanting to help those people is ingrained in them at birth. Some people may be empathetic, but they may not show it as much because they sometimes find it difficult to put themselves in another's shoes or understand the emotions of another individual. Coping with overwhelming emotions as an empath can seem impossible at times because when you feel another's emotions so strongly, it feels like you are suffering from their emotions. Empathy can help you connect with other people and make friendships that last a lifetime, but it can also hinder you because of how draining it can be to be around people who are always complaining and never happy. Being an empath is a blessing, and a curse all rolled into one; being an empath means that you care deeply about others, but it also means that you feel the emotional stress of those around you sometimes more than your own. Some empaths practice a few activities or hobbies to channel their energies into something positive instead of focusing on negative things all the time. Here are some of them:

Reading

Books are a good escape for sensitive souls because they can get lost in a fictional world or learn something new while relaxing in their favorite chair. They can read about anything they choose and feel satisfied when empaths finish a good book as if they had accomplished something great. Allocating a few hours for reading can help empaths recharge their energies from all the emotional stress they experience daily. Reading helpful articles and self-help books such as this can help empaths better cope with their situation.

Listening to Music

Like reading, listening to music can relax a sensitive soul and help them get through hard times by escaping into someone else's world through music. Certain musical frequencies have been found to help in coping with physical pain and mental stress. The repetition of music helps the brain reach a state of relaxation, similar to meditation and yoga, but without the stretches or poses. Empaths tend to listen to music to maintain their balance and relieve the tension in their body and mind. Some music also urges you to get up and move around, which helps relieve stress and negative energies. Listening to uplifting music can help you cope with negative energies and assist you in finding a positive perspective on your life, especially if you listen to your favorite songs over and over.

Learning New Languages

Empaths often find themselves lost in their world of thoughts and problems; however, learning a new language can help them become more socially active. Language studies help your brain obtain new neural pathways that help you develop critical thinking and improve memory skills. By learning a new language, an empath can increase their ability to focus and deal with everyday life issues more calmly and effectively.

Photography

Most sensitive souls are drawn to capturing memories and storing them in their memory banks forever. Picking up a camera and becoming involved in photography is a satisfying hobby for sensitive souls because it captures the beauty of the world around them and helps them feel emotionally fulfilled through the memories they create. Photogenic memories can trigger an emotional response, and empaths are inclined to capture every beautiful moment in life through their camera lens. Photography teaches you how to appreciate the beauty of the world while you practice controlling your emotions at the same time.

Cooking

Some people are just born to cook; others are gifted with the ability to make delicious meals whenever they feel like it. For empaths who find cooking a relaxing activity, it's a great way to take their minds off their problems and focus on something productive instead. Empaths who love to cook can also pass on their skills to their loved ones, like their friends and family, and they can use this talent as a career in the future if they wish to.

Watching Movies
Movies are fun to watch because they can provide entertainment while also teaching viewers something. Sensitive souls might enjoy watching comedies because they tend to be more lighthearted than dramas and are usually happy stories. Empaths can also learn valuable life lessons from watching movies, helping them feel more optimistic when they watch these positive movie genres. Some movies can also become informative and can help you as an empath to become better acquainted with other sensitive individuals' stories.

Writing
Writing or journaling is another outlet for an empath to express himself or work through feelings without confronting anyone directly about their bottled emotions. It also helps you get to your "happy place" when writing about positive things in your life or a letter to a loved one. Writing is also good because it can be an escape from your everyday life and allow you the time to relax while still doing something productive at the same time. Poetry, book writing, or calligraphy writing is another way of channeling negative emotions into something productive and positive. These activities can help sensitive souls organize their thoughts and release emotions by writing them down on paper or blogging online.

Focusing on Art
Drawing or other mediums of art can help sensitive souls gain control over their frustrations and their need to express their feelings constantly. Art therapy can help an empath release negative energy into creativity instead of letting it build inside and cause further distress. Art can be a great outlet for healing empaths. Creative painting, drawing, sculpting, and other art forms can allow an empathic person to express the emotions that they are feeling through color, texture, and shape. Many

artists have claimed that when they paint, they feel a surge of creativity that helps them feel relieved from stress and anxiety. Painting gives people a way to express themselves without saying a word. Art is a form of therapy that can relieve the stress of everyday life and allow artists to feel calm. It gives them a way to unwind and release their feelings of exhaustion, anxiety, and stress without physically hurting anyone in the process.

Gardening

Gardening or walking in nature can be a relaxing hobby for sensitive souls who have a green thumb and need to get away from everything to clear their heads and relax simultaneously. Spending time outside in the fresh air while gardening can put the mind and soul at ease and help relieve stress. Gardening for empaths is therapeutic because of the healing power of plants and the calming effect it has on their body, along with removing negativity from their surroundings. Growing flowers, herbs, vegetables, or even a small yard garden can help reduce stress levels. It also helps your soul recover from the emotional stress you face every day by focusing your energy on growing beautiful flowers and vegetables instead. It is a form of meditation and teaches patience and perseverance as the plants grow and thrive over time. The plants and flowers add various patterns and colors to your environment, which can cheer you up as you look around.

Exercise

Another healthy outlet for sensitive souls who need to burn some energy or release some pent-up frustrations they may be feeling about someone or something else in their lives is exercise. Sometimes a little exercise is all an empath needs to regain their inner strength and get over some difficult days, weeks, or even months that he may be having emotionally. Exercise tones not only the body but also the mind. Being active helps clear the mind of all negative thoughts that cause mental distress and physical illness. Being a highly sensitive person comes with a lot of responsibilities, but being aware and mindful about the way you handle your emotions can make all the difference in the world. Your emotional health is just as important as your physical health; both are equally important when it comes to living a healthy life and enjoying life to the fullest.

Maintaining a Healthy Lifestyle

Along with exercise, eating healthy is another way to keep your body and mind healthy by nourishing your cells properly so they can grow and remain strong. Eating junk food contributes to poor mental health and can even trigger symptoms of depression and anxiety in some people. Drinking lots of water keeps your body hydrated, keeping your energy up, your mood stable, and your concentration clear. Staying active throughout the day can help boost the immune system as well.

Engaging in Healthy Social Activities

Keeping yourself occupied and being social keeps you busy and helps you maintain a positive attitude about life, which can be quite difficult when you are an empath who feels things deeply. Having an active social life, volunteering your time to help others, being involved in charitable events, spending time with family and friends, or other kinds of social activities can help you cope better with difficult situations you face as an empath.

Traveling

For some empaths, travel is refreshing and helps them recharge their batteries while learning new things about different cultures worldwide. Others, on the other hand, may find it stressful because of not being able to control the emotions of others they encounter while traveling. It is important to remember to protect yourself while traveling to avoid feeling overwhelmed by negative emotions that are within. Bringing your solitude kit, a series of items that helps you become solitary in chaotic surroundings that I have referenced in Chapter 6, can come in handy as you travel to different places should you need it.

Massage Therapy

Highly sensitive people often suffer from tension and headaches from stress, so a good massage can help relieve tension and calm the mind, body, and soul. Massage therapy also helps release any negative emotions that may still be trapped inside the body and the mind, which can be very therapeutic for empaths. Targeted massaging, such as acupressure and deep tissue massages, alleviate and eliminate stress. It can also help regulate sleep patterns for an empathic person.

Getting Enough Sleep

having ample rest, just like recharging is important to your social energy, is essential to being productive and energetic the next day. It can also help you cope with difficult emotions and feelings better. Sleep enhances the brain pathways, and for empaths, whose minds are always running like a race with a thousand thoughts racing through their mind at the same time, resting can be a much-needed break to recharge their spiritual energy again. Learning something new. Learning something new every day keeps your mind and body sharp, which helps you stay mentally healthy and alert as you grow older. For highly sensitive people, learning a new skill like a new language or playing an instrument can boost their confidence and make them feel better by mastering a new skill they may not be good at yet.

Meditation

Meditation is a way to center yourself, release negative energy, and gain balance. There are many different techniques for meditation. Empaths, also known as highly sensitive people, constantly experience feelings of turmoil. These emotions cause them to feel overwhelmed and irritable. When faced with stress, they typically experience some type of emotional episode. Meditation can help empaths cope with their feelings of overwhelm and frustration by giving them a sense of peace and clarity on how to handle these situations differently next time around. A good guided meditation can help an empath learn deep breathing techniques and improve their mood effectively without experiencing any negative side effects. Through meditation, an empath can become more aware of the situations that cause them distress and help them avoid situations that trigger their emotions negatively. A certain form of meditation known as mindfulness meditation can increase self-awareness and create deep connections with others. This technique encourages empaths to become aware of their thoughts and actions while simultaneously calming the mind and body.

Positive Visualizing

Empaths can practice imagining and manifesting how they want to feel when they feel happy as they wake up and start their day. They can imagine they are on vacation with a loved one or taking a long drive alone to clear their minds and take their minds off of their stressors in life, even if it's just for a few minutes at a time. Our minds only identify thoughts and have no distinction between what is positive or negative. Visualizing events and situations positively eliminates the chances of negative thoughts and emotions entering your mind, which can help you maintain your emotional balance.

Reciting Positive Affirmations

Affirming yourself, also known as a mantra, helps release some of the negative energy you are feeling and helps shift your focus in a more positive direction. You can use affirmations when angry, sad, frustrated, etc. Mantras can come from repeating positive words or phrases that resonate with you. Your affirmation should be short and simple so that it can stick with you longer throughout the day. Repeating your affirmation in your head whenever you think of it can keep your mind focused on positivity and help you cope with negative feelings of anxiety or depression. Working out to release negative emotions in the body. I have included positive affirmations that can help you boost your self-esteem and help you feel better mentally, spiritually, and physically, especially when feeling down.

There are more ways for you to cope with their bustling environment according to your liking. No matter what you choose to do to recoup your energy, remain focused and positive in everything you do so you don't fall back into negative thinking patterns and become overwhelmed easily. You can constantly feed your mind with positive details to help yourself become more emotionally balanced and maintain a positive outlook on life as you grow older. Your empathy is a superpower that only a few people only have.

Chapter 7: Preventing Empaths from Emotional Overwhelm

When you are an empath, you feel everything everyone else is feeling. Sometimes every little thing feels fantastic and uplifting; other times, it feels like a drag and a drain. Sometimes you get so caught up in other people's emotions that your feelings get ignored, suppressed, or buried completely. This event can cause you to become exhausted and depleted of energy quickly. Being an empath means you are naturally highly sensitive to other people's energy, so their moods, feelings, and intentions can strongly affect your well-being and energy. As a highly sensitive person and an empath, you are naturally more sensitive to emotional and energetic shifts than the average person. Here are some tips to help you feel balanced at all times.

Eat the right food.
Healthy food makes an empath feel better emotionally as well as physically. Avoid eating too much sugar and processed or fried foods because they make your body acidic and make you sick to your stomach. Eat only organic foods as much as possible and avoid processed and refined foods. Avoid processed foods whenever possible; they are full of chemicals that cause the body to feel drained all the time.

Junk food can also make empaths gain weight and cause other health problems like diabetes or high cholesterol. Drink plenty of water: Water helps the organs in the body to function well, including the kidneys, liver, and colon. These organs help keep your mind clear from negative thoughts and help you be more positive and happy. Dehydration can lead to headaches, fatigue, poor digestion, irritability, and more.

Cleanse your aura.

There are plenty of guided meditations for aura cleansing readily available on music and social media platforms that you can listen to when resting or before you sleep. Search "Guided Meditation" on your browser and see various meditation techniques. Listening to these videos and audio files can help to clear your mind of negativity and help you to sleep better at night. While listening to any guided meditation, you can do these steps:

1. Set a timer for your preferred length in minutes, then find a quiet and comfortable place to sit down.
2. Close your eyes and breathe a few times deeply to relax your body and calm your mind.
3. Visualize a golden light surrounding your body from the tail of your spine. You can visualize this light as a golden glow or a white light flowing through you to the top of your head.
4. Imagine that the light is healing you and is removing any negative energy from you. Visualize this negative or stagnant energy as black smoke slowly being cleared from your aura. Continue deep breathing while visualizing the clearing process until the timer goes off.

Protect yourself from others' energies.

Empaths are prone to negativity and can be overwhelmed by what is happening around them. Empaths must protect themselves from other people's negative energies by staying away from those affected by negative emotions. Protect yourself from harmful energies by wearing protective stones such as:

- **Amethyst:** for protection from psychic attacks. Amethysts are healing stones that attract calming energy to the bearer and protect them from negativity and other negative influences. Empaths benefit from amethysts for their soothing properties and the protection it provides from absorbing other people's emotions and energies.
- **Black tourmaline:** for protection from electromagnetic frequencies that can harm you mentally, emotionally, physically, spiritually, and even financially. This stone is also good for grounding and protecting you from radiation emitted from electronic devices.
- **Citrine:** helps you feel more empowered and protected simultaneously; it is a stone of abundance and helps increase your self-esteem and confidence. Empaths can wear citrine jewelry for balancing your chakras and keeping your energy field strong and protected.
- **Obsidian:** empaths can benefit from obsidian by wearing it as a pendant around their neck; it can protect you from collecting negative energy from others and maintain your energy balance. You can also place it under your bed or near your electronics to absorb electromagnetic frequencies and protect yourself from WiFi and other electronic waves that are harmful to your health. Minimize contact with toxic people: Toxic people are those who hurt you mentally, emotionally, or physically with their words and actions. When you are around these people, you can feel drained instantly just by being near them.
- **Clear quartz:** are powerful amplifiers of energy and can be cleansed by placing them in sunlight or moonlight overnight. This stone amplifies energy and your intentions. It also helps to restore balance and clear your aura from stagnant energy. Wearing clear quartz pendants can help keep the aura clear of negativity,

stress, and anxiety caused by other people's energies. How to be grounded:
- **Jasper:** a stone said to provide nurture and support during stressful times. Jaspers can help empaths in releasing fear and anxiety by releasing the negative energy trapped in their chakras. It also helps to prevent empaths from collecting negative energy from other people by grounding their energy fields.
- **Blue lace agate:** absorbs and neutralizes negative energy from your environment and releases positive energy into your space, which helps to balance the positive and negative aspects of your life. Blue lace agate is also helpful in reducing stress and making you feel calm and relaxed.

Consult with your ancestors or spirit guides.

Some meditations guide you to speaking with your ancestors. It is a way that you can connect with your roots and see the way forward to your destiny path. Speaking with your ancestors helps empaths heal from their emotional traumas and deal with their past emotional pain. It is a powerful way to discover your past lives and your purpose in this lifetime. Some ancestors can become your spirit guides and can help you with your spiritual journey in life. You can meditate to connect with your ancestors and ask them for help and guidance. This step can help calm you down and remove unsettling thoughts from your mind. You can follow these steps:

- Find a quiet place where you can comfortably sit down or lay down.
- Close your eyes and focus on your breathing. Feel your heartbeat as you breathe in and out slowly and deeply until you feel calmer and more at peace. Remember to

- breathe regularly without straining yourself to do so. Listen as it slows down and becomes steady.
- Imagine standing in front of an old tree in the middle of a lush meadow with a river flowing nearby. Visualize the sound of the water gently rushing and the wind gently rustling the leaves and branches.
- Imagine that you are standing with your ancestors who are sitting under the tree, patiently waiting for you to speak. Your ancestors may remind you of people in your life who no longer walk with you on this journey through life, and they may also remind you of those who still walk with you. Ask them to give you advice and wisdom on moving forward on your life path. Ask them to show you the way ahead in life.
- Listen to their advice intently and spend time with them to enjoy the calmness of the area. When you have finished talking to your ancestors, thank them for their presence, guidance, and wisdom, and then thank the tree and the river for their calm presence and peaceful energy that surrounds you in the area where you meditated.
- When you feel ready, open your eyes and write down whatever guidance you received from them in your dream journal or on a piece of paper.

Consulting with your spirit guides or ancestors can help empaths heal themselves from their emotional wounds and prevent them from constantly feeling drained due to constant exposure to other people's negative emotions and energy fields. This practice is how they can protect themselves from being energetically drained and protect others from being affected by their toxic energy and emotional turmoil.

Ground yourself.

Energy is all around us. Everything that is living has energy in it, including us humans. Every action we take and every thought we think creates some type of energy around us that can affect those around us or even spread beyond it to affect a larger group of people or even the whole world. We, humans, are sensitive beings who are highly attuned to the energy around us. Sometimes we feel drained for no apparent reason, which is when we need to ground ourselves again. Being grounded means connecting to the earth so that we can recharge our energy by taking in positive energy from the earth and expelling negative energy from it. This step is how you can restore the balance in your energy system and help yourself feel more energized and balanced again. Grounding also helps us to feel more connected to the earth. Earth energy is where we draw our energy from, which helps keep us balanced.

Grounding is important to empaths to protect them from absorbing other people's negative energies and emotional turmoil. For empaths, being grounded is like unplugging themselves from electric sockets to avoid being electrocuted when using electric appliances. It helps them keep their energy systems balanced and clear, so they can function normally without feeling drained or emotionally unstable. To ground yourself:

- Imagine a giant metal rod going through the center of your body into the ground below you, connecting you to the Earth's natural magnetic field.
- Feel your body become anchored to the ground below you and feel a strong flow of healing energy from the Earth entering your body through your feet, traveling upwards to your head.
- Allow this healing energy to rejuvenate your body, soul, and spirit and heal any past wounds inflicted upon you by others due to situations beyond your control.

- Imagine the energy flowing through your entire body to rejuvenate and restore your energy balance. Now feel this same flow going outside your body and into nature, which is absorbed into the Earth's electromagnetic field.
- Feel all the energy in your body being absorbed back into the Earth itself, clearing it of all negative energies and pollutants. Feel yourself becoming lighter and stronger; feel your energy level returning to normal.

Practice grounding yourself as often as possible throughout your day whenever you feel your energy drained from your body, usually towards the end of your day. Grounding helps us to feel more energized, balanced, focused, and alert, so it's best to do it often.

Another type of grounding is **walking barefoot on the earth.** It helps empaths to ground themselves further and draw even more healing energy from the Earth into their bodies to replenish their energy reserves. To walk barefoot on the earth:

- Find a grassy field, park, forest trail, beach, or other natural area where you can walk barefoot on the ground for at least 15 minutes.
- Stand still and listen to the sounds of nature around you: birds chirping, the wind blowing through the trees, shore waves crashing, the rain pattering on the ground, and let these sounds and sights comfort you and relax your mind, body, and spirit.
- Walk barefooting or use a walking stick to feel the earth beneath you. As you feel your bare feet connect with the earth, feel the soothing vibrations beneath your feet, the cool grass against your skin, and smell the fresh scent of the trees or the salty ocean air. Feel how your body becomes more relaxed and peaceful as your mind and body reconnect with the Earth and her positive healing

energies. Use your senses to feel the subtle energies that affect your body.
- Breathe deeply and walk slowly, stretching your legs and spine to prevent injury or pain; proceed gently and calmly.
- Thank the earth for helping you to heal from all past emotional wounds caused by others through situations beyond your control, and feel all the negative energies released through the soles of your feet into the Earth's electromagnetic field, where they are absorbed into the earth itself and are cleared of all negative energies as positive energy is restored to Mother Earth.

Empaths need to learn how to release their negative feelings and energy blocks whenever they feel emotionally overwhelmed to prevent themselves from feeling uncomfortable and stressed. This can help you to stay grounded, balanced, and relaxed all day. It's best to release all negative emotions when they first arise to prevent them from accumulating within our bodies and causing us to feel more drained and emotionally unstable than usual. The feeling of sadness and anxiety is the most common emotions experienced by empaths. When they occur, it's important to release them right away before they can build up inside our bodies and cause us to self-actualize the pain physically, from headaches to muscle strain to other sicknesses.

Consider how many times you have disregarded your gut feelings. These instincts are what empaths rely on to self-protect from negative energy manipulation from others. Anytime you feel uneasy or uneasy about a situation or person in your life, listen to your intuition and pay attention to your feelings. If you feel like you're being manipulated or controlled in some way by someone else in your life, it may be time to let go and move on from them so that you can heal your emotional wounds from the past and begin a new life where you can begin again. If you have trouble letting go, you may wish to consult a therapist to assist you in resolving any issues preventing you from letting go of toxic relationships in your life.

Remember that as all good things come to an end, life continues. You may find that you have difficulty trusting people after you've experienced bad relationships. If so, you may want to explore ways to build healthy relationships based on trust and respect for others. Remember: it's okay to trust again; it's okay to trust yourself. Make time for yourself each day to relax and clear your mind from all the stress you've been experiencing. Take time to meditate and be alone without anyone except for your pets.

Your pets are there for you.

Allow your pets to give you unconditional love and comfort. Your pets might ease the stress and restore your energy balance. Let your pets restore your faith in humanity by showing you that there is still good left in the world, and allow the unconditional love of your pets to help you to let go of all the negative feelings and energy blocks stored in your heart. Pets can help you let go of all past experiences and emotional wounds inflicted by others because of circumstances beyond your control. Let yourself heal and remind yourself that you are not alone.

Empaths tend to keep their pets at bay for emotional support. They give empaths the strength to feel confident about themselves again, to know that they are not alone in the world and that they will always have the love and support of their pets and the Earth's compassionate energy to help them heal from the pain of the old and welcome the future filled with happiness, joy, and peace. Allowing your pets to love you unconditionally can give you hope and help you feel stronger and more empowered. Your pets will always be there for you when you need them most. Pets can help empaths ease their troubles and give them the courage to face the world.

Release your strong emotions.

Think of yourself as a glass full of water. When it is full, it overflows. Empaths are very sensitive to overwhelming emotions. When they are emotionally overstressed, they may cry a lot. When an empath cries, tears are released, and the negative energy is released back into the earth, where it is absorbed. Once stored within the earth itself, it is purified of all negative energy and released as positive energy back to Mother Earth, restoring peace and harmony to the environment once again. Empaths must release their strong emotions and cry as much as they need to balance their emotions and restore the harmony of their environment.

Don't be afraid to cry and release all the pain and negative emotions you've been holding in for so long. Crying can help relieve your pain and allow your strong emotions to be healed by the loving energy of the Earth itself. Simply relax as you feel all your negative energy being released, cleansed, and cleared away. Visualize this occurring as the earth absorbs all the negative energy stored within your body, clearing away all the pain from the past so that you can begin anew, reborn into a new life filled with happiness and joy. This emotional cleansing process can be highly beneficial for both you and your environment as a whole. Take a deep breath and close your eyes as you feel the negativity being absorbed and released back into the ground around you. With your negative thoughts, feelings, and emotions released, you'll feel a sense of peace that will help you feel relaxed and rejuvenated.

Some empaths release their emotions by screaming at the top of their lungs or punching a pillow to release the stress that has been building up inside their bodies. Do whatever works for you to release your stress and restore the energy balance within your body by releasing your pent-up stress and negative emotions from your body. Release your fears about not being good enough or strong enough to be a good person and help those around you heal their wounds and heal themselves.

Believe in yourself and trust in yourself as you allow others to heal their emotional wounds and embrace a new beginning for themselves. Wish them well in their new journey in life, and let go of any negative feelings you have toward them as you send them healing thoughts to help them heal. Do not focus on negative aspects of other people's behavior; focus on the fact that you are a good person with good intentions who is doing your best to help others heal emotionally from the pain of the past and help them embrace a new beginning filled with happiness, joy, peace, and love for themselves and others around them. If you cannot let go of negative experiences from the past due to past traumas and abuse you may have experienced in your life, seek the help of a professional counselor or therapist to help you work through your emotions and heal your past hurts once and for all. Empaths must always believe in themselves and have faith that they are doing everything they can to help themselves and others around them heal from the emotional wounds of the past and welcome a fresh start for them in the future. Never give up on yourself or lose hope in yourself. No matter how bad things get, there is always hope to be found deep inside you if you dig deep enough to find it. Always remember that you have your own back and never let anyone take advantage of you or make you feel small.

Chapter 8: Finding Comfort in Confusing Places

This generation is constantly bombarded with conflict, and empaths are especially vulnerable. "I see and feel your pain" is one of the most common phrases we hear as an empath. However, it is a phrase we sometimes have trouble saying to ourselves or those around us. Most of us have been conditioned to think that showing our emotions is a sign of weakness. We are trained to bottle up our feelings so that we don't seem "too emotional" or so that we don't get "too upset." This approach does not work, and you end up bottling up so much anger that it explodes at the worst possible moment.

So how can you allow yourself to feel your emotions without feeling like you're going to burst? Take some time alone to decompress and relax after a traumatic event. It is completely normal to be sad or upset after a traumatic event, but take some time for yourself to calm down before you reach out to someone to help you heal. Take time to be with your feelings; don't push them away or ignore them because you feel you should.

You can feel your emotions as natural reactions to trauma instead of ignoring them and trying to get rid of them. You don't have to take your feelings out on those around you; you only use your emotions to your benefit! As humans, we naturally seek comfort and love from others, and we are naturally attracted to people who make us feel good. Use this to your advantage by reaching out to the people in your life who make you feel good.

Good Experiences Will Do You Good

Look around you, for plenty of good things are happening around the world. Empaths enjoy the events where emotions run high; they are attracted to the positive energy that flows during happy occasions. If you enjoy being around people during happy times, find places where many people gather together in celebration.

Spend time with people who enjoy being around you, and seek places where you can surround yourself with positive energy. Family and friends that support you can play an important role in your healing; make sure you're surrounding yourself with the right people. After trauma, it's important to allow your body's natural healing process. Your body is always trying to heal itself; sometimes, you need to give it time to work its magic. The human body is composed of more than 100 trillion cells, and each has a powerful immune system that works to repair and heal the body from the smallest injury to life-threatening illnesses.

Participating in marathons can help empaths cope with stress and recharge their social batteries at the same time. After participating in a marathon, an empath often feels recharged and ready to deal with any challenges life throws. Exercising helps to release endorphins that give us a sense of happiness and well-being. If you're feeling stressed, take a walk outside and get some fresh air to clear your mind; this can clear your head and release tension in your body. Empaths are often rewarded with intense energy when they exercise; this energy can further help you cope with life's constant drain.

Choose What You See on Social Media
Screening what content you consume on social media can help empaths recover from trauma and maintain a healthy and balanced lifestyle. It is easy to get caught up in the drama of social media drama; however, focusing on negative stories will only drain your energy and create anxiety. Instead, use social media as a positive tool to find inspiration and motivation. Encourage others by sharing positive stories on social media; this can keep you motivated and focused on what makes you happy in life. Although tragedy is an inevitable part of life, an empath can take steps to heal from trauma and prevent future pain.

An easy way to filter your content on social media is to unfollow pages that continuously post negative stories and engage in arguments in the comments. By limiting your social media exposure, you can focus on healing from past tragedies and on moving forward in your life. Another way is to choose which content you wish to see. If you choose to see funny or happy content, you can decrease your exposure to negative posts significantly. Sometimes the hardest part of dealing with stress is figuring out what is causing it in the first place. Your best resource when trying to reduce stress is yourself. Once you've identified the cause of your stress, you can take steps to deal with it more effectively. Filter the people who have access to your energy. This step can seem drastic, but releasing yourself from toxic relationships is necessary to move forward in your life. Create boundaries with toxic people so that they don't continue to drain your energy; you should practice "no contact" when dealing with toxic people.

Additionally, do not attempt to fix other people; spend your time and energy focusing on your healing and happiness instead. Avoid negative people and environments. If negativity consistently surrounds you, it can cause you unnecessary stress and anxiety; remove yourself from situations that cause stress and take time to relax at home instead. Surround yourself with positive people. Choose your friends wisely, and make sure you spend time with people who make you feel good about yourself. Positive people can help you focus on things you can be grateful for in life, for they can push you forward to achieving your true potential. These people can be family, friends, relatives, mentors, or even colleagues.

In cases when you are already overwhelmed by all that is happening, you can preserve your energy by taking breaks or limiting content from family and friends. Social media can be a great resource for inspiration and motivation; use this to your advantage by choosing to follow pages that post inspiring and positive stories. Focusing on positive stories encourages you to think positively about your life and promotes self-care. Instead of stressing over other people's problems, you can find inspiration and encouragement through inspirational quotes or uplifting stories on social media. By sharing positive stories and encouraging others, you can help spread positivity in the world. When people are feeling overwhelmed by stressful situations, it's easy to give up or give in; however, it is crucial not to lose hope when struggling with a difficult experience.

Social media can help empaths spread positivity around them by sharing their uplifting story and inspiring others to overcome their struggles. Promoting positivity through social media is a powerful tool that can help encourage and heal others while promoting self-care and self-motivation at the same time. Some empath groups share their healing journey with others on Facebook and other social media platforms to connect with others and share stories of healing together. Sharing your story with others through social media can bring both healing and inspiration; this is a great way to heal while also inspiring others to pursue their healing journey. Supporting and encouraging others is one of the most rewarding things you can do for yourself and others. When you support and encourage others, you are allowing yourself to be vulnerable; this vulnerability allows you to connect with others on a deeper level.

As confusion wrecks the lives of those around them, empaths are frequently thrown into extreme physical and emotional turmoil. They are naturally inclined to be emotionally vulnerable and tend to be deeply intuitive. It is rare for an empath to be only one or the other; they may alternate between being emotionally driven and driven intellectually. Converting it to positivity can help you as an empath to not only cope with situations but also make them work for you. When an empath is in a negative space, they can use negativity to their advantage by using their intuitive nature to discover the best course of action to take; this is where their sense of optimism can help them heal from the trauma of life's most stressful moments. Life has its ups and downs; there is no right or wrong way to cope with these ups and downs. If an empath feels as though their life has been turned upside down, there are things that they can do to cope. The body and mind are constantly working to heal themselves, and as much energy an empath has lost, they can replenish it by focusing on self-care and healing from past traumas. Being empathetic means recognizing your pain in others and helping those in pain by comforting them in times of need. Adversity is not something that comes solely from the outside; adversity often comes from within. Adversity forces people to look inward and understand where the source of their problems lies; this understanding can help an empath heal from their pain and move forward positively.

Be the Change You Want To See in Others

Empaths can bring a message of happiness and optimism to this world. They are meant to heal others and often find themselves drawn toward careers where they can make a positive difference in the world. During times of hardship, consider making a positive difference.

Volunteering at a homeless shelter is a great way to lift your spirits and help others at the same time. There is always something good happening somewhere in the world; you simply have to look for it. You have the power to help change the world as an empath, and in doing so, you become a powerful symbol of hope and joy for those around you. For empaths, motivating change in others is second nature. You sense what other people need and want even before they do, and you help them realize that they can get there by changing their perspective and taking action steps to help them achieve their goals. An excellent approach for empaths is to give back to your community by volunteering, which is ideal for plenty of reasons. It fosters interpersonal connections, encourages selflessness, and provides a chance to serve those in need. By volunteering your time and talents to others in need, you can release some of the burdens on your shoulders while making a positive difference in the lives of others at the same time.

Being an empathetic leader means inspiring others to follow your lead and become positive forces for change in their lives. As an empathetic leader, you inspire others to change their lives for the better. You give people a reason to believe in your vision and motivate them to take action steps toward their goals. As a leader and empath, it's your job to help others get what they want out of life. You are never powerless. You have what it takes to become the best version of yourself, and you deserve to be happy. All you need to do to start making positive changes in your life is to learn the art of manifestation, understand your empathic abilities, and then put yourself out there in a way that allows you to thrive.

Some empaths participate in fundraisers to give back and help those in need. There are many organizations and causes that you can support as an empath; find one that speaks to your heart and get involved. Through these contributions, you can make a difference in the lives of those around you. By helping others, you become a source of strength for them, and they can feel the positive spirit you radiate from deep within your soul.

Participating in events as a volunteer can help empaths liven up their community spirit with others. When you volunteer for a cause or an organization, you can gain new experiences and meet new friends, possibly, even new connections. Volunteering can teach new skills and give you something to look forward to regularly. Even the simplest act of service can brighten someone's day and let them know they are loved and appreciated. Volunteering is a great way to meet like-minded people and develop meaningful relationships with new people in your community and worldwide.

Encouragement is key to helping others reach their potential and become the person they want to be, and empaths are often great sources of encouragement for others. Empaths can feel what another person feels and understand their point of view; this is a wonderful gift that allows you to help others through their struggles or tough times. If you can relate to others' feelings, you can offer words of comfort and support to people in need, which is a great trait for just about anyone to have. Encouraging others makes an enormous difference in their lives; they know that you are there for them, no matter what obstacles they may face in life.

Perform One Random Act of Kindness Daily

Random acts of kindness can bring empaths great happiness, and they will often do one random act of kindness every day to bring joy into the lives of others. As an empath, you have a unique ability to tap into other people's feelings, and this can help you better understand their needs. You can perform random acts of kindness by leaving encouraging notes for others to find, volunteering your time at a shelter or soup kitchen, or donating clothes and other items to those in need. You create a ripple effect through random acts of kindness. You can create a ripple effect that can positively touch many lives. Sharing your positive energy can inspire others to do the same.

Helping others out is one way that empaths can help themselves; another is to focus on changing themselves for the better. Performing acts of kindness can be good for you because it makes you feel better about yourself; however, it's not the only way to improve your own life. Strive to be your best self every day by making positive changes to your health and life goals. Every new change you make can positively affect your life, and you will be rewarded with a lifetime of health and happiness. As an empath, you can sense other people's emotional needs; however, your feelings often get lost in translation along the way. Helping people out would make you feel much better about yourself; this way, you can learn to communicate with others in a way they can understand. Practice active listening by asking questions and understanding their answers.

As an empath, you're born with the ability to comprehend and experience the emotions of others. As a result, you're naturally inclined to be compassionate and understanding of others. You are inherently gentle and cooperative, and many people find you very gentle and soft-spoken. Your ability to communicate effectively with others is your greatest strength. This gift can help you make random acts of kindness to others by helping them understand that you care about them. Your kind heart and intuitive nature help you make people feel heard and understood, and you can help them realize their worth and potential in life. Empaths bring harmony to the world through their warm, generous, and nurturing natures.

As a healer at heart, you always seek to uplift the spirits of others. You are a symbol of hope and compassion to those around you, and you strive to make the world a better place through your selfless acts of service and kindness. You give love freely because you understand as an empath that giving and receiving love is a two-way street; when people open their hearts to you, you also open yours to them in kind. Open yourself up to the good vibrations of love that constantly surround you. When you feel tired or drained of energy, tap into the loving energy surrounding you. Focus on being grateful and appreciate all of the blessings you receive each day; this helps you get through the day more peacefully and allows you to experience greater happiness as an empathetic being.

There are many other ways to center yourself in confusing times. This step may differ for each person, but for empaths, it can be as simple as lighting a candle and focusing your thoughts for 10 minutes on just one thing you are grateful for at that moment in time. It can also just be waking up in the morning, having a meal, having a nice shower, or even seeing your pet cat lying peacefully next to you as you relax on the sofa. Simple moments are all you need to center yourself on again and remember what you love about life. Enjoy each moment of life as it comes. Each moment is precious; when you realize this, you can enjoy it more fully. When you focus on the good things in your life, you thank the universe for all the good things you have. When your cup is full, you can spread happiness and positivity to others. Practicing gratitude brings more joy into your life; you will feel more fulfilled knowing that you have much to be thankful for. This positive outlook allows you to enjoy yourself more fully and enjoy everything life offers, including the ups and downs that come your way from time to time.

As an empath, you experience the power of the dark side, also known as negative emotions. You are naturally compassionate and wise. You are naturally inclined towards helping other people and influencing them positively. With all of these traits, you can steer your life to use your compassion and achieve harmony. There are also plenty of good things happening in the world, and empaths are lucky to be part of it because they can shine a light into the darkness. The dark side may be a challenge, but this challenge is also an opportunity for an empath to realize his full potential and be of service to others. By accepting your dark side with grace, you will be rewarded with fulfilling your goals as a wise and compassionate individual. Empaths can use their gifts to help make the world better by creating peace in their hearts and in those around them. Positively use your compassion and empathy to serve humanity and realize your full potential as a wise and compassionate human being.

Chapter 9: Career Path for Empaths

People with empathy frequently struggle to find work or the right career and take on too many responsibilities. Self-care is incredibly important for an empath as they need to take time out to rest and relax. Otherwise, they will become exhausted and unable to function effectively. But an empath's brain doesn't differentiate between a good or bad feeling, so they will often feel responsible for other people's feelings and well-being as well as their own.

As an empath, you're often highly motivated and idealistic. This energy can help you push yourself further and reach your goals at work but can also lead to burnout when you don't balance it with rest. Machines even crash when they are overworked, and empaths are no different.

Empathy in Many Types of Work

Empaths at work are sensitive and perceptive and have a distinct personality type. This trait comes with its challenges and gifts. While empaths by nature are gifted with great compassion, it has also led to self-doubt and anxiety. However, through meditation and other mindfulness practices, empaths can tame their nature and harness its power for good intentions. You can look for a profession that complements your talents, abilities, and personality. To determine whether a job is a good fit, use your gut. Once you use your empathetic abilities in your career, you will begin to excel in your chosen field and achieve success.

As empaths like to communicate over the phone, via email, or text message, they prefer to work alone, in low-stress positions, or for smaller businesses. These traits show how respectful they are of others' personal space and also mean that they don't like to be around many people at once. As an empath, you are intuitive and easily pick up on the emotions of those around you. You tend to care deeply about others' emotions and well-being because you experience everything intensely yourself. You are empathetic and compassionate towards others which means that you are willing to put yourself in someone else's shoes to understand how they feel.

Self-employment is another way for empaths to avoid being overwhelmed by coworkers. They enjoy working for themselves more than working for a large company or organization where they must deal with constant interruptions from superiors and colleagues. Being an empath makes you self-aware and more in touch with your emotions, and this, in turn, makes you more sensitive to the sentiments of others. It also means that you can sense when something is wrong or when someone is upset or angry, even if they haven't said anything to you about it yet. Working alone or with only a few people means you are less stressed because you are aware of what is happening around you and are prepared for it. It can also help you to make better decisions and avoid problems before they happen. If you're self-employed, you may consider working as an editor, writer, artist, or another creative career. You may also think about careers concerned with protecting the environment and ecosystems.

Empathy and Creativity

As one of the most common jobs available to people who love all things creative, it's easy to understand why arts and entertainment can be thrilling for empaths. Since expressing emotions is not an empath's strong suit, they tend to gravitate toward artistic careers where they can express their emotions artistically rather than verbally express to others. If you are an empathic introvert who prefers to work independently than with others in a group setting, you may want to consider a career in arts. Performing artists can express themselves freely on stage or in front of the camera without worrying about how others may perceive them. These individuals are often multi-talented and enjoy taking on multiple roles within the arts industry, such as acting, writing, directing, music production, and more. You can turn your passion for the arts into a fulfilling career that allows you to use your creative skills to inspire others and create art that others can enjoy. Because many artists work solo or in small groups, they can work when and where they want without a lot of interruption from colleagues. Art galleries and art schools can also be great places for introverted empaths and artists to network and meet like-minded people and similar or shared passions. Empaths are commonly natural artists as they enjoy creating things for others to enjoy and appreciate. Many find that they have liked painting and drawing from a young age and are very passionate about their work. They typically enjoy the process more than the outcome and find fulfillment in creating something beautiful from a blank canvass. Graphic design is another popular artistic job for empathic people as it involves using images to communicate a message and express emotion. A graphic designer can create logos for companies or advertisements that help sell a product by appealing to consumers' emotions. Fashion designers are also great jobs for empathic people as they can express their creativity through their clothing designs which appeal to various audiences. These individuals often create clothing that reflects their personality and tastes, making them successful in this industry. Many fashion designers also create their clothing lines or work for well-known brands as a designer for a specific line within their company.

Always a Helping Hand, Even at Work

Empaths enjoy helping others and working in healthcare or social work where they can make a positive difference. They also find fulfillment in teaching and mentoring others because they love to teach and share their knowledge. Other professions that resonate with them include counseling, psychology, education, medicine, veterinary science, hospitality, and media communications. Many choose to work in these industries because they are passionate about humanitarian causes such as animal rights and the environment. On the other hand, empaths need to take regular breaks to meditate and concentrate on themselves since they can't take on the symptoms and tension from others. Those empaths working in the medical field often experience high-stress levels because of their work's emotional intensity and empathy for their patient's feelings. When working with empathic people, it's important to understand that your coworkers might not always be able to express their emotions appropriately due to their empathy for you. This situation may lead to misunderstandings, making it difficult for you to work together effectively on a project. It's important as an empathic person to work with other empathetic people who understand your sensitivities and can respect them.

Careers that Empaths Avoid

Because empaths pick up on other people's tension and emotions and are frequently bothered by commotion and bright lights, sales occupations are not enjoyable. Any sensory overload can confuse them and cause them to feel disoriented or anxious. Many avoid working in loud environments such as restaurants, bars, factories, etc. Additionally, they might feel drained after a day at the office and may find it difficult to focus on anything other than taking a long nap to recharge their social batteries. They may take frequent breaks throughout the day to relax and re-energize themselves, which can affect their performance at work.

Working in a corporate setting can also cause empaths to feel overwhelmed because of their exposure to many different types of people throughout the day. When working in this environment, they should take frequent breaks from the office to de-stress and relax in their free time to return to their work feeling refreshed and ready to tackle the day ahead. Being empathic also means you have a high pain tolerance and can endure pain better than most people without being emotionally overwhelming. Some empaths seek a career in the healthcare industry or any other profession that requires lots of physical labor. However, this means you are prone to fatigue and other health problems if you push yourself too hard physically without taking time to rest and recover. It would help if you also were careful about letting your empathy get the best of you and prevent you from doing what you need to for yourself to stay healthy and strong on the job. As empaths are independent thinkers, they may find bureaucracy in the corporate world suffocating and slow-paced jobs boring and unfulfilling.

Mental stress can break empaths into sickness. And while highly stressful careers like law and politics are highly rewarding and can become a humanitarian movement for empaths, it can also break them down emotionally to the point where they are mentally exhausted and often suffer from depression and other mental health problems. Since they can be intense, people with high-stress jobs often experience difficulty expressing themselves. Some also experience post-traumatic stress disorder, or PTSD, from witnessing violence or other traumatic events, resulting in panic attacks or other mental disorders that make it difficult for them to function normally daily. Empaths may find themselves avoiding social situations where they will have to deal with large crowds of people as they might find it too much to handle emotionally, to which lawyers and politicians may normally be exposed. It does not mean that empaths cannot handle the level of intellect and focus these careers require; they only must revitalize whenever necessary.

Empaths in Leadership Roles

People feel comfortable confiding in empathetic leaders because they know their abilities, which makes them great for leadership and coaching positions. This trait helps you relate to your staff but might make you dislike confrontation. Empaths are compassionate leaders who see the bigger picture beyond their own needs and focus on their team's goals instead. As a leader, you should maintain an open-door policy where your employees are free to discuss any issues with you without fear of reprimanding or disciplinary actions. By allowing your employees to speak freely to you, you can help them overcome their issues and be more productive in the workplace. As a leader, it's your responsibility to make sure your employees feel safe enough to voice their opinions without fear of repercussion. Your staff members rely on you for guidance and direction, and you should establish yourself as a trustworthy leader who is not afraid to offer support in times of need. Treating your team with kindness and respect will inspire them to reciprocate the same kindness to others around them. Your employees are like family to you; therefore, you should treat them with the utmost respect and kindness as you would your own family, which comes naturally for empaths.

There may be times when your employees take advantage of your empathic leadership ways, and you must make sure to establish boundaries to protect yourself from emotional exhaustion or burnout. Sometimes you may have to discipline an employee who disregards company policies for personal gain or behaves inappropriately in front of others; however, you should be sensitive to the fact that you are an empathetic person who cares for others' feelings and concerns. Taking disciplinary action against someone you care about is difficult, but protecting yourself from employees disrespecting you or your team is important. Here are a few tips to help you manage your team:

1. **Reviewing the details.** Disciplinary actions can cause empaths to retreat into themselves and avoid engaging with their team members; however, as a leader, you must stay objective enough to deliver a fair and just punishment when necessary. Set clear boundaries for yourself by reviewing the details of the situation before delivering your decision to the employee in question. It will allow you to remain focused during meetings and maintain your composure during discussions. Empaths deliver details positively to their team members for problem-solving purposes; therefore, you should view disciplinary meetings as an opportunity to solve issues among your team rather than delivering negative news to them. Remain positive and calm while speaking with the employee in question. Never raise your voice or become defensive while addressing the situation; instead, remain calm and explain to the employee the severity of their actions and the possible consequences of future misconduct. Keep your emotions in check, and do not allow yourself to be overcome by the situation at hand.
2. **Consult your company's guidelines.** This step can help you as an empath in leadership; it allows you to refocus on the situation at hand to provide an objective response that will satisfy all parties involved in the disciplinary process. Taking a step back from the situation allows you to consider all factors involved in the incident before deciding on an appropriate punishment. For instance, if an employee is caught stealing office supplies for personal use, you should first consult the company's guidelines on appropriate

workplace behavior to determine whether or not this act grounds a disciplinary action.
3. **Stay true to your cause.** Let your employee know you understand their situation and respect their opinion, but remind them that their actions affect the entire team negatively and must be corrected immediately to prevent further problems from occurring in the future. As an empath, you can help your employees understand the objective of the disciplinary action by speaking to them one-on-one and providing them with the support and resources they need to improve their performance. Empaths tend to care deeply about the welfare of their employees, so sometimes, you may find it difficult to terminate an underperforming employee. You should remind yourself that you are a team leader; therefore, it is your responsibility to set a good example for your employees and encourage them to do better by example. This step can also help them understand why the disciplinary measure is necessary, as it will allow them to reflect on their behavior and determine if their behavior needs to change in the future.
4. **Be firm yet fair in your decisions.** This trait will allow you to avoid feeling responsible for your team member's actions or emotions after making a decision. Encourage open communication between yourself and your employees by setting up regular meetings to discuss important company issues or projects your team is working on. Empaths can guide their team to greater success by inspiring them to work harder to achieve goals. They should, however, remember to take the right steps to protect themselves from experiencing mental exhaustion that could lead to burnout. Feeling tired after a long day at work is normal; however, feeling tired every day after work may be a sign of

mental exhaustion and may affect your work productivity.
5. **End the conversation with a positive note whenever applicable.** You should understand that as an empath, being upset about the outcome is sometimes expected. It is not your responsibility to console your team members after they have violated company policy; however, you can still end the conversation on a positive note by expressing gratitude for their contributions to the organization. Also, thank them for taking the time to meet with you and share your concerns. Dismissing them abruptly without showing any empathy will make them feel worse about the situation, which will affect their performance and overall happiness in the workplace. Take the necessary steps to protect your mind while ensuring your conversations with your employees are well-handled.

In a bustling and hustling environment, empaths thrive by managing their emotions appropriately and effectively to ensure successful interactions with your team members. The unending patience empathetic leaders have can motivate and inspire their team members to do better; therefore, you should use the traits you possess to inspire success among your team.

Chapter 10: Center Your Empathic Self

Even though empaths prefer to be alone, they are always a part of the mix and are open to the energy around them. You, as an empath, must practice centering yourself in unpredictable situations to allow yourself to handle your energy better. Since you are highly sensitive to the energy of others and their environments, you can sense other people's feelings easily and intuitively feel their energies. This ability allows you to help others feel better when feeling down or sad. However, this ability can also become a problem in an empath's life if they constantly pick up on the energy of those around you.

Losing balance of your emotional needs can be problematic for empaths since they can take on other people's energies too much and begin feeling overwhelmed and drained. Therefore, empaths must learn how to manage their energetic sensitivity to maintain their energy and mental health. Empaths should try to balance their empathic abilities by learning to shut off their feelings for others' emotions and energies. One way to do this is by finding an activity that you like to do that will allow you to focus on yourself rather than on the energy around you. When immersed in your favorite activity, you may be less sensitive to the energy around you and will feel less drained after spending time alone. In addition, you may become more aware of the emotions you are feeling and can then learn to control them in a way that doesn't cause you to absorb others' energies. To gain control of your empathic abilities, you must learn to focus on your well-being first to help other people find their balance.

Center Yourself

Centering helps you regain your power and results from applying awareness and attention to return to a normal state. Highly sensitive souls need to center their energies regularly by practicing techniques to help them feel more grounded. In today's hectic world, you may feel more overwhelmed than usual. As a highly sensitive soul, you have extra senses and gifts that others do not have. But it is important to take care of your needs to take care of yourself in stressful situations, and to keep yourself centered and balanced. Centering for empaths has helped them in challenging situations, such as being in a crowded environment or with someone whose energy may overwhelm you. When you feel over-emotional or overwhelmed by someone's energy, take the time to center yourself by grounding and focusing on the present instead of worrying about the past or future. Staying centered can help you remain calm and balanced. While learning to stay centered can be challenging, you can slowly develop these skills with practice. You can also learn techniques to help you stay centered, such as deep breathing or energy visualization.

Your energy reacts to what you do or say each time. Keeping the balance in your energy allows you to react calmly and avoid conflict during conversations and interactions with others. Centering involves balancing your emotions, thoughts, and energy. Your emotions do not determine who you are; they tell you where you are at any moment. These feelings can help you decide how to react and manage your behavior in certain situations. Once you have mapped out how you can find balance, you can center yourself whenever you feel overwhelmed by your emotions or affected by others. Giving an equivalent reaction to others' actions makes empaths overwhelmed, but you can find ways to manage your energy and emotions while dealing with them. Taking time for yourself will allow you to gain control over your emotions and help you deal with difficult people and experiences. The hardest thing for an empath is learning to manage and control their emotions, for they can easily be overwhelmed. Empathy is normal to be easily upset and even depressed when faced with challenging situations and people. As an empath, you often feel things very deeply and can sense trouble a mile away. Use this to defend yourself from what can affect you negatively.

For example, when another person is upset with you or you feel angry, you can use centering techniques to overcome negative emotions that prevent you from being productive in your daily work life or relationships. As a highly sensitive individual, you react quickly to your surroundings and feel every emotion around you. These reactions may be positive or negative and can be triggered by anything from a loud noise to an intense conversation. Take time to learn ways to ground yourself by resting your body in comfortable positions and finding quiet places where you can focus your attention on your thoughts and surroundings without distraction.

Another way is to take deep cleansing breaths. This method is done to relax your body and calm your racing mind. Here is how you can do it:

- Close your eyes. Clear your mind of any thoughts. Focus on your breath for 2 minutes.
- Visualize a beautiful, serene scene in your head with all of nature's sounds around you. Then, imagine that all of the things you see are glowing with energy. Your feet will glow with your energy and gently pulses as it goes to the earth and back to your feet.
- Imagine the pulsing light on your feet wrapping your entire body and overflowing from the top of your head like a fountain of energy. This energy goes back to the world's core as it lands on the earth.

- Focus on your breathing and take deep breaths as you become present and self-aware. Feel the air going in and out of your lungs as you inhale and then exhale slowly. You can stay as long as you can.
- Remember to do these steps as you feel your emotions overwhelm you.

Another way of centering is envisioning a place that makes you feel good, peaceful, and relaxed. It can be anywhere you like: a forest, a beach, a meadow, or a garden. It could be a room in your house where you like to be alone. Follow these steps:

- When you go there in your mind, imagine yourself in your favorite place, relaxing in a hammock, or sitting by the fireplace with a cup of your favorite drink in your hands.
- Take a deep breath and focus on clearing your mind of any thoughts. Meditate on how you want to feel in that moment and place.
- Take another deep breath and thank the Universe for all the blessings it gives you. Once you're ready, you can return to your awakened state.

Any energy management exercise's primary goal is to help you concentrate on your aim. Your ideas and intentions control your energy field, and it responds to everything you say and do. Empaths are prone to taking on other people's emotions and negative energy because they also absorb other people's energies. To relieve stress, focus on what you want to achieve in life, accept what you cannot change, and be positive about it. To release negative emotions such as fear, anger, frustration, anxiety, depression, etc., you can use the techniques above.

Set reminders to center yourself daily. You can practice it in the morning before going to work or in the evening before you go to bed. If you are having trouble controlling your emotions, schedule a meditation session every day when you spend time for yourself. Find a way to center yourself when you feel negative emotions coming on during the day so you can manage your emotions rather than let them take control of you. You will be surprised at how much better you feel when you learn to center yourself and release negative emotions from your body and mind.

Calling Divine Forces

Some empaths ask help from divine forces to center their energies and find balance. A good example is Archangel Michael, the protector of planet earth. He also guides people spiritually and gives guidance to those who are confused and need help making decisions in their lives. He can protect your soul from negative energies and any external dangers that could threaten your life journey and help you keep your energy and spirit balanced and calm during emotional situations. You can ask for him anytime to help you protect yourself from negative feelings: Here's how you can call on the Archangel Michael:

- In your quiet time, close your eyes and clear your mind.
- Use the same phrase: "I call on Archangel Michael to protect me from all negative energies and give me guidance so I can make the right decisions in my life." Call on him three times during the day and night before you sleep.
- When you feel yourself getting angry or confused, you can repeat the same phrase three more times until you feel calm.

As empaths, we get energy from every person we meet and everything we experience. It's easy to feel overwhelmed by this energy. But by learning to manage your emotions, you can protect yourself from absorbing negative energy from the environment and other people. Release negative and unnecessary emotions, and release or protect your energy from negative energies. Learn to refocus and gain clarity when you're feeling confused or overwhelmed. Empower yourself with positive intentions to channel your energy in the right direction and experience more good things in your life.

If you can't find the time to center daily, you can do a quick reset at any time of the day by focusing on your breath for a minute, feeling the light radiating from your feet into the earth, and then back again to your feet. These steps will help you to center yourself and re-energize after a stressful day. Then, you can meditate and relax before going to sleep to center your energy field before going to bed at night. For a good night's sleep, you can listen to a guided meditation on stress management using an app at bedtime. When you wake up in the morning, you will feel energized and ready to face the day ahead. Remember that being sensitive can be a gift as long as you learn how to control your emotions so you can manage your behavior in any situation and remain balanced and peaceful throughout your day.

Consciousness to Unconsciousness

If you have practiced the centering technique for some time but are still having trouble, you may need to identify the issues preventing it from working. Blockages can happen to empaths in their thoughts, feelings, body, and spirit due to past traumas, current situations, or old beliefs that no longer serve them. Regularly practicing these simple centering exercises can help you regain balance in your energy field by decreasing your sensitivity and increase your self-awareness. It also helps you notice when your energy is out of balance. Empaths who have mastered centering themselves can recharge their batteries faster so they can feel more energized throughout the day. Practicing these techniques makes you feel calmer and centered at all times. Life will be easier for you as a highly sensitive person when you can manage your reactions to situations and respond appropriately to the actions or words made by others. Your unconscious self can help your empathic abilities by slowing down your thoughts so that you'll only focus on one thought at a time instead of worrying about dozens of things at once. If you worry too much and feel exhausted at the end of the day, try to slow down your thoughts and practice centering techniques to regain your energy so you remain grounded and balanced throughout the day.

Guilt can cause empaths to feel overwhelmed and confused because it doesn't usually feel right for them to do certain things or have certain thoughts. Highly sensitive people often feel guilty for not living up to people's expectations or being emotionally unavailable to others because of their own needs. Guilt can also come from their actions - feeling they are not doing enough or being judgmental of themselves or others. While empathy can cause many difficulties for empaths, guilt makes it even harder for them to overcome their condition and live a balanced life. However, there are ways for empaths to deal with guilt:

- **Understand the feeling.** Negative emotions can stem from shame, fear, unworthiness, or regret. You may feel guilty for something you did or did not do in the past and feel remorseful for causing harm to others. You may have pushed someone away that you cared about even though you had good intentions at heart because you wanted to be independent. Or you may have helped someone without fully considering their feelings and made them feel uncomfortable because you assumed you knew best. Understanding the emotions, you're going through can help you become conscious of them so that you can realize why you are feeling this way and identify possible solutions. Identify the cause. When you understand why you feel guilty, the next step is to identify the source of it. It can be your choices, decisions, actions, behavior, attitude, reactions, etc. It may be something you did to yourself or someone you hurt knowingly or unknowingly that has caused you to feel guilty. For example, you may feel guilty for not spending time with your family because you were working overtime to meet a deadline and didn't realize how much time you had missed. Once you have understood where your guilt is coming from, acknowledge that you could have done things differently and avoid making the same mistakes in the future. Forgive yourself for the things you have done wrong in the past. Letting go of past mistakes can be painful at first because it reminds us of the hurt and pain we have caused ourselves and others. However, when you realize you are human and have made mistakes, it will be easier to forgive yourself and move on with your life.

- **Enjoy your alone time.** Empaths should not be empathetic all the time. Building boundaries can help empaths to enjoy life without worrying about others' problems all the time. They can do it by spending time alone to recharge their batteries, enjoy nature, meditate or do yoga, or lie down and rest after a busy day. They also find value in spending time with like-minded friends whose company they enjoy more than spending time with others to be sociable. Sometimes, it can even help empathetic people to listen to their favorite music or read a book for a couple of hours without feeling obligated to be with people all the time. Avoid people who drain your energy. Having lots of friends who are different from you can be a blessing and a curse to an empath because you need different kinds of energy every day. It can help keep you from being drained by

other people's energies but having too many draining friends can affect your mood and energy in the long run. Feeling guilty about having alone time is normal for empaths, and you shouldn't feel bad about that. After all, your need for quiet and solitude helps you stay balanced in your life.
- **Find ways to be of service and when to avoid them**. Offering your empathic gifts can make you feel fulfilled and happy about yourself. If you need to help someone, you have to find a way to do that without being overwhelmed by their energies. Find a way to make yourself feel good and share it with others so they can benefit from it as much as you do. Becoming a crying shoulder to a friend can make empaths feel like they are losing themselves in the process because they feel they have nothing left for themselves. They may then feel guilty for not taking care of themselves the way they want to. Co-dependency can happen to empaths due to extreme fear of abandonment and low self-esteem. They struggle to take care of themselves because they want to be needed by others, so empaths won't feel rejected if they get rejected. However, if you're in a public place, don't look directly at the 'energy vampire' – observe their body language with peripheral vision, or try to shift your focus elsewhere, like a book or your drink, while pretending that they are of no interest to you at all.

Reach out to the Pros

If you are struggling to find peace within yourself and feel unable to manage your own emotions, talk to a professional counselor who can personally help you work through it. There are meditation gurus that specialize in healing and spiritual guidance that can help empaths overcome their condition and develop tools for managing their emotions better. Working with a life coach can also help you learn how to deal with your empathic abilities more positively so that you don't feel depleted at the end of each day.

Apart from facing guilt, you can also have your chakras cleared by a trained spiritual healer to balance your energy centers and rid yourself of negative emotions that can hold you back from fulfilling your true potential. Chakras are seven energy centers in the body that govern different facets of our personality. Blockages in these chakras can lead to health issues like anxiety, depression, digestive issues, back pain, etc. For instance, the heart chakra deals with love and relationships, and an imbalance in your heart chakra can cause you to become envious of someone or depressed. Being empathic can affect your chakras negatively if you are not in balance emotionally or spiritually. Spiritual healers use crystals and energy healing methods like Reiki to balance these chakras and release negative energy from the body. Balancing your energy centers can help align your body, mind, and spirit and helps release feelings of negativity from within you so that you are better equipped to deal with everyday life stressors. Understanding your emotions and what they tell you can help you better deal with them and improve your well-being.

These steps above are only a few of the many ways that an empath can center themselves. It can differ from one person to another. Once you have found the method that works for you and centered yourself, you are ready to move forward on your journey of self-discovery as an empath.

Chapter 11: An Empath's Healthy Diet

Highly sensitive souls tend to push themselves harder to balance their energy constantly. With their continuous struggle, choosing the right diet is important for empaths to maintain a healthy emotional well-being. Choosing the right diet helps an empath to reduce stress and increase positive energy.

Here are some items of food for empaths to boost their energy levels and overall health:

- Salmon is one of the best fish to eat for a healthy heart as it is rich in omega-3 fatty acids, which help reduce inflammation in our bodies. It is also known as a great mood booster and an energy booster as it contains vitamin B12, which helps to boost our energy levels as well.
- Oats are also good for energy as they have a good amount of protein, which gives our body the energy it needs to perform daily functions. It also has fiber that helps maintain the level of blood sugar in the body and keeps us feeling full for longer periods.
- Raw fruits like apples, blueberries, oranges, pineapples, pears, and bananas are great snack options for empaths as they are full of minerals and vitamins that help to lower cholesterol. These fruits have antioxidants, which protect the body from free radicals that cause cell damage in our bodies. They also help to keep our immune system strong.
- Green tea is a great stimulant as it boosts the immune system and improves brain functions. It also improves

metabolism and helps with weight loss. It also helps with sleep problems as it relaxes the nervous system and calms the mind down.
- Dark chocolate is good for our moods as it contains phenylethylamine, which triggers the release of endorphins in the brain, boosting our moods.
- Almonds and other nuts are a good source of vitamin E and protein, which help to keep our brains healthy and improve memory retention. They also contain magnesium which helps with muscle cramps and other health issues. They are also high in monounsaturated fats that help to reduce blood pressure and protect our hearts from strokes.
- Avocadoes are considered a good source of fat as they help lower cholesterol and prevent heart diseases. They also help to lose weight as they are low in carbohydrates but high in fiber.
- Beans and lentils are very good for heart health as they improve circulation and contain folic acid, which helps with depression. They also have protein which helps build muscles. Brown rice is rich in iron, which helps with anemia. It is also full of fiber and complex carbohydrates, which help you feel full for longer. It is also good to control blood sugar levels in the body.
- Healthy oils such as olive oil or coconut oil are beneficial for health as they contain healthy fats, which improve blood circulation and help lower cholesterol levels in the body.
- Leafy greens such as spinach or kale are also good for our health as they prevent cancer and boost the immune system. They are also high in iron and help boost our energy levels.
- Chia seeds are high in protein, calcium, potassium, and omega-3 fatty acid, which is good for the heart and brain.

- Quinoa can help empaths control their stress levels as it is packed with magnesium that helps calm nerves and lower stress hormone levels in the body.
- Tomatoes are a good source of lycopene, an antioxidant that helps protect the body from free radical damage that can cause chronic diseases such as cancer and heart diseases.
- Carrots are a good source of vitamin A that helps to maintain the health of our eyes and skin.
- Mushrooms have vitamin D, which helps prevent autoimmune diseases and inflammation. They are a good source of vitamin B, which helps improve concentration and reduces fatigue. They also have selenium which protects us from infections and helps detoxify our bodies.
- Turmeric has curcumin, an anti-inflammatory agent, and helps fight infection in our bodies. It helps to heal wounds faster and also prevents stomach ulcers.
- Cinnamon is good for the brain as it increases dopamine levels, making us feel good and happy.
- Ginger is good for digestion as it has anti-inflammatory properties and helps soothe the digestive tract.

Keep in mind that there are other healthy food items that you can add to this list. As an empath, you can determine which items suit you best by paying attention to how you feel after eating them or eating them regularly over a while.

Chapter 12: Good-to-Know Stuff for your Empath Child

Your kids are likely to experience some troubling emotions. They're also likely to be curious and adventurous. As parents of empathic children, you strive to make parenting easier for them. Kids are naturally empathic and sensitive but may struggle to cope with their world. Your child's world is full of change, especially when they begin school. As a result, your child is likely to feel confused or anxious in a new situation or environment with unfamiliar people.

For example, your child may struggle with feeling sad when a friend moves away. This overwhelming feeling can slowly take away their social energy over time and end up leaving them in sadness. This chapter will help you identify if your child is an empath and how you can help them manage their energies early on in life.

How to Identify an Empath Child

Empath children are easy to spot because they feel intense emotions quickly and tend to cry easily. You can distinguish empaths by how they react to various life situations. Here are some of them:

- **Empath children might get upset easily.** As young ones are still figuring out emotions and how overwhelming they can be, these kids are likely to be more upset than their peers when they're hurt or disappointed about something, like getting in trouble at

school for misbehaving or their sibling breaking their favorite toy.
- **Empaths tend to have vivid dreams that seem real to them at times.** They may dream of someone and feel like they've met them before in real life or that their face appears on television later on. They may not be afraid to talk about their dreams or interpret them to those around them. Their dreams may be symbolic of how they are feeling at any given moment, such as when a dream is about losing something or someone important in their life.
- **Another sign of an empath child is their ability to sense when someone is upset or even depressed.** They also tend to easily pick up on other feelings such as anxiety, anger, fear, and surprise. They don't just absorb these feelings from other people around them; they can even sense them from a distance as if someone is in the same room with them. These kids are often highly sensitive and can feel what others are feeling at a moment's notice.
- **Empath children will often seek physical closeness when upset or need comforting because they are aware of their feelings.** They will wrap their arms around their parents for reassurance, even when they lie on the sofa watching cartoons together. Similarly, they may also have a hard time separating from their parents when they need to fall asleep at night. This trait can easily cause sleep deprivation for empaths because parents are usually too attached and want to sleep with their kids until the kids are ready to fall asleep on their own.
- **Empath children also have great intuition and can usually tell when something is off in a room, even if others don't notice anything is wrong**. They may notice that a door is ajar, a lightbulb is out, or a closet is

open even though others haven't noticed it. They usually point out these things to their parents, who will appreciate it because it will make their home safer or more secure. However, their intuitive abilities may also make them appear to have a "sixth sense" of other people and circumstances. Their sixth sense allows them to pick up on the subtlest emotions or sensations around them.

- **You may also notice that your kids' strong empathy towards animals makes them more compassionate.** They will rarely hurt a fly in their room and will become protective of their friends too. They can feel the feelings of those around them and care for others. When a child shows empathy toward another kid in their class who is being bullied, they will stand up for them and defend themselves against the bully. They may feel angry and resentful toward bullies because it offends them deeper than most kids, and they may believe that everyone should be kind to others.
- **They may question why some kids may be unkind to other kids and why bullies are allowed to act that way. It may not seem fair, which is why parents need to teach their children to be kind to others.** Empath children can be one of the most compassionate around them. They are more aware of others' feelings and encourage other kids to be more empathetic toward others too.
- **Empathic children feel lonely more often than other children; they have a deep connection with people and are always around people, so they crave solitude at times to feel relaxed or get away from the hustle and bustle around them.** They would rather stay at home alone than hang out with friends because they prefer a quiet and relaxing atmosphere. While home alone, they will daydream, relax, read, and

watch television because they are introverted and enjoy spending time alone without people bothering them. They are generally shy and usually feel more comfortable in one-on-one situations.
- **Your child may have trouble dealing with transitions;** they might feel afraid when faced with something unfamiliar, and as empaths, they feel their emotions deeply, so they tend to feel frightened more easily than others. They are observant and pick up on the smallest details that are out of place and may constantly worry about their safety.

Helping your Empath Child Manage Emotions

Your child's brain is wired to empathize with others by recognizing their distress and offering comfort or support to help them cope. However, this empathy can also be triggered when your child observes others in distress without directly experiencing it. This emotional reaction is known as alexithymia, where a child can find it hard to identify their own emotions as separate from someone else's and even more difficult to convey them to others. As empath children progress in life, they gradually learn to handle situations better and become more resilient to stress. They also learn to notice what other people around them are feeling and offer help when they need it most. The following tips can help your empathic child:

- Allow them to express their emotions. Empathic children are naturally compassionate individuals. They tend to show empathy towards their peers or family members through simple gestures like:
    - hugging them
    - holding hands
    - listening to their problems without judgment

- saying thank you when necessary
- Write a diary to help you remember your parenting attempts. Keeping a journal on how you support your empath child can remind you of past experiences that may have helped them develop empathy later in life. You can revisit these journal entries if your child experiences a challenge in the same situation and refer to how you helped them at the time.
- Encourage them to make friends with others their age. By spending time with other friends, they can learn how to develop stronger friendships with peers as they grow older. You can also teach them how to react to negative emotions in different situations and offer support and comfort when needed.
- Empath children feel all of the emotions around them. Being upfront and honest with your empath child is important; don't hold back on the truth because you think they won't understand it.
- Set boundaries for their behavior. Empathic children are great listeners and tend to take on other people's problems as their own. Although this tendency can be very helpful at times, it can also cause them to be easily affected by others' negativity and stress. You can help your child develop their boundaries by setting rules for interacting with people outside the family. You can also encourage them to find a hobby they enjoy to keep themselves busy and develop their interests further.
- Set a before-bed routine for your child. It is one of the necessary things to help maintain your kids' health, as it gives them a sense of safety and order over their lives. You can use this time to discuss their day and teach them about new emotions and feelings they may have encountered that day. For example, you may ask them to explain how they felt upset when a friend didn't invite them to a party, how someone may have bullied

them at school, and how you didn't let them get to you that day. You can also offer reassurance that they can rely on you if they ever encounter a similar situation in the future. Empaths tend to have difficulty falling asleep due to anxiety, which can also happen to children. These steps can depend on what works best for your child to help them fall asleep. A good routine may include:
- Taking a warm bath
- Brushing their teeth
- Changing to pajamas
- Tucking them to bed
- Ask them one new thing they learned during their day
- Reading a bedtime story for them
- Good night hugs and kisses

- Encourage their creative side. An empathetic child's creative side tends to thrive when they feel calm and relaxed. Set aside time in the day where they can do arts and crafts, read a good book, or play their favorite video game. Letting your child participate in creative activities allows them to release their stress and engage in an activity they truly enjoy while developing their creativity further.
- Observe how your child reacts to situations. Being an empath has its ups and downs, especially when your child grows up in an emotionally unstable environment like your home. Your kids are likely to have a tough time expressing their emotions openly to you. Because they can sense other people's feelings easily, they may feel left out whenever you're busy dealing with your issues at work or home, and this may lead to loneliness, anxiety, and depression in the future if they don't find a way to express their feelings to others around them.
- Inform your child that while you appreciate their help, there may be times that you will handle things

separately as they are too young to become involved in adult matters. Tell your kid that mommy and daddy have things under control, and you will ask for help when needed. Whenever they lend a hand, show them your appreciation by thanking them or doing something special, like cooking their favorite meal or taking them out for ice cream.

- Your empathic child can become upset with loud noises or crowds. Make sure to listen to their needs as you bring them to crowded places, such as shopping malls or movie theaters, so they don't feel overwhelmed or stressed out. You may also take breaks from visiting crowded places from time to time to give them a chance to recover and feel calm again. You can give them a safe space in your home to relax and unwind on their own while letting them healthily deal with their emotions. Encourage them to be gentle with others. Being empathetic can be difficult to teach a child, especially when they're constantly exposed to aggressive and violent behavior from others around them.
- Practice mindfulness with your kids to help them manage stress better. You can begin by teaching them deep breathing exercises and remind them that they can do these steps when there is too much going on around them. You can also help them by distracting them from situations when their emotions get the best. Explain to your kids that meditation is not a magical pill that will take away all their problems; instead, it is a tool that will help them healthily deal with stress by controlling their emotions, thoughts, and actions more effectively.
- Set a time limit for using devices. Children with higher levels of empathy tend to spend a lot of time on social media or playing computer games; this can cause them to develop addictive behaviors in the long run. Talk to your kids about how much time they are spending on

their devices and help them identify activities that can help them manage their time better instead of wasting it playing video games or chatting online with friends. Create a list of hobbies and activities they can try when they feel like they want to relax instead of turning to social media or video games.
- Teach your kids how to say no in a respectful manner. Because they're natural-born caregivers, it may be difficult for your child to say no when someone they care about is asking for help or favors. Give them tips on communicating what they need from you without hurting anyone's feelings. Remind your empath child that it is okay to say no from time to time so they can focus on their own lives too. While empathy and compassion are admirable traits, they can also affect your child's mental and emotional well-being. Always remind them to take care of themselves first before taking care of others around them.
- Take them to see their family doctor or pediatrician regularly for check-ups and discuss any concerns you may have regarding your child's health. Never ignore their mental and emotional symptoms if they experience anxiety, nightmares, or difficulty sleeping, as this may be a sign of depression or post-traumatic stress disorder, or PTSD. Hidden and untreated illnesses can cause your empath child to feel overwhelmed and depressed when they grow older. Talk to your pediatrician about your concerns for your child, so they can diagnose the problem and provide treatment immediately.
- Be there for your kid when they need emotional support or guidance. Encourage your empathetic child to share their feelings and concerns with you, whether it's during lunch, family time, or in the car when heading home. Remember to reassure them that they can always

approach you with their problems. As an empath parent, you can teach them to become more aware of their emotions and how to ground themselves when needed.

59 Positive Affirmations

Positive affirmations express the belief that a certain thing is possible. They can benefit anyone striving for a goal by teaching them to think positively. Some people read positive affirmations every day to achieve specific goals. You can benefit by repeating these simple statements to yourself to help you overcome negativity and succeed at your goals.

Repeating positive affirmations help you reach any goal you strive for by increasing your self-confidence, building a positive attitude, and boosting your determination. This helps you visualize your goal and realize the importance of reaching it. This can be any goal you have on your mind!

Affirmations can help you reach your goals faster as they are positive thinking. They involve repeating a phrase or statement until it becomes "second nature."

Now relax and calm down as you repeat each affirmation five times in a row for 2 minutes each. You will listen to the affirmation, and there will be a pause of 2 minutes after each affirmation to give you enough time to repeat the affirmation and let your brain process it.

59 Affirmations for Empowering Empaths

1. I am confident.
2. I am a warrior and a winner.
3. I can bravely face my challenges.
4. I can heal and move forward.
5. I am secure in my strength.
6. I am courageous.
7. I feel empowered with a wealth of resources and support, including my Higher Power.

8. I am confident, secure, and empowered.
9. I am a beautiful person.
10. I am happy and hopeful.
11. I am helpful.
12. I grow and thrive.
13. I have faith in the future.
14. I am peaceful, loving, and kindhearted to others and myself.
15. I am generous with myself and with others.
16. I am confident, secure, and powerful.
17. I have overcome my trials.
18. I help others to be strong and confident.
19. I have faith in myself and others.
20. I feel the positivity of the world around me.
21. I am grateful and abundant.
22. I am in harmony with the world around me.
23. I am strong and capable.
24. I am filled with light and love.
25. I am powerful.
26. I help others, and they rely on me for direction in life.
27. I am strong and secure in my abilities, my talents, and my worth as a person.
28. I am humbled.
29. I believe in miracles and possibilities for new and better things to happen in my life.
30. I am part of the world around me.
31. I am connected to people and things in this world that I love and appreciate.
32. I can manage my overwhelming emotions.
33. I let go of old negative patterns and habits that no longer serve me well.
34. I practice self-care and nurturing.
35. I help others to have the confidence to move forward in life.
36. I believe in myself.

37. I am brave in becoming who I am.
38. I have successfully overcome adversity and strife.
39. I feel safe, loved, and hopeful.
40. I am an integral part of becoming a better world.
41. I can channel my energy to help others.
42. I am ready to forgive myself and others for past mistakes.
43. I am at peace with myself and my life in the world around me.
44. I am compassionate and loving to others and the earth I live on.
45. I am grateful for my past and experiences, which have shaped me into who I am today.
46. I am open to new opportunities in my life.
47. I accept myself as the unique person that I am.
48. I am one with the world.
49. I am a part of nature, the cosmos, and the forces that lead me to what I want in my life.
50. I am perfectly okay with who I am as a person.
51. I accept that my soul is a work in progress and that I will grow and transform as my soul unfolds.
52. I am part of a beautiful world whose people love me.
53. I have become more grateful for the amazing people in my life, living in a world where peace predominates.
54. I am surrounded by the warm and caring presence of those who love me unconditionally.
55. I am grateful for the love and support of friends, family, and community.
56. I understand the spiritual world around me.
57. I find greater meaning in my life.
58. I am joyful and thankful for everything in my life and the people around me.
59. I am my Highest Self.

FREEBIES

AND

RELATED PRODUCTS

WORKBOOKS
AUDIOBOOKS
FREE BOOKS
REVIEW COPIES

HERE

HTTPS://SMARTPA.GE/MELISSAGOMES

Freebies!

I have a **special treat for you**! You can access exclusive bonuses I created specifically for my readers at the following link! The link will redirect you to a webpage containing all my books and bonuses for each book. Just select the book you have purchased and check the bonuses!

>> https://smartpa.ge/MelissaGomes<<

OR scan the QR Code with your phone's camera

Bonus 1: Free Workbook - Value 12.95$

This **workbook** will guide you with **specific questions** and give you all the space you need to write down the answers. Taking time for **self-reflection** is extremely valuable, especially when looking to develop new skills and **learn** new concepts. I highly suggest you *grab this complimentary workbook for yourself*, as it will help you gain clarity on your goals. Some authors like to sell the workbook, but I think giving it away for free is the perfect way to say **"thank you" to my readers**.

Bonus 2: Free Book - Value 12.95$

Grab a **free short book** with **22+ Techniques for Meditation**. The book will introduce you to a range of meditation practices you can use to help you develop your inner awareness, inner calm, and overall sense of well-being. You will also learn how to begin a meditation practice that works for you regardless of your schedule. These meditation techniques work for everyone, regardless of age or fitness level. Check it out at the link below!

Bonus 3: Free audiobook - Value 14.95$

If you love listening to audiobooks on the go or would enjoy a narration as you read along, I have great news for you. You can download the audiobook version of *my books* for **FREE** just by signing up for a FREE 30-day Audible trial! You can find the audio versions of my books (depending on availability) at the following link.

Join my Review Team!

Are you an avid reader looking to have more insights into spirituality? Do you want to get free books in exchange for an honest review? You can do so by joining my Review Team! You will get priority access to my books before they are released. You only need to follow me on Booksprout, and you will get notified every time a new Review Copy is available for my latest release!

For all the Freebies, visit the following link:

>> https://smartpa.ge/MelissaGomes<<

OR scan the QR Code with your phone's camera

I'm here because of you 🖤

When you're supporting an independent author,
you're supporting a dream. Please leave an honest review on Amazon by scanning the QR code below and clicking on the "Leave an Amazon Review" Button.

★★★★★

https://smartpa.ge/MelissaGomes

Printed in Great Britain
by Amazon